Discovering Your Psychic World

Reading People · Sixth Sense · Predictions · Meditation · Stress Relief · Sending Colors · Clair-audience · Sending Emotions · Remote Viewing · Reading the Aura · Sending Symbols · Dreams · Visualization · Sending Pictures · Automatic Writing · Dowsing · Psychometry

by Annette Martin

illustrated by Bruce Pettyjohn

Artistic Visions, Inc.

PUBLISHERS NOTE

Discovering Your Psychic World

ISBN 1-885764-01-4

Published by Artistic Visions Inc.
2075 Winchester Blvd. Suite 107
Campbell, CA 95008-3432
408-378-1435

To my
loving husband
Bruce
and students

without whose assistance and encouragement
this workbook would never have been written.

Contents

Contents

Foreward

by Penelope K. Hogg, Ph.D.

Having been a teacher since 1966 and a clinical psychologist since 1986, I was well aware of the developmental process, the learning curve, and strategies used to maximize our abilities.

Knowing this, I wanted to develop more seriously my intuitive skills. It was synchronistic that I had mentioned this to a trusted colleague and clinical psychologist, Dr. Paulette Jacome, indicating that I was searching for a master teacher in the intuitive arts, someone who was "grounded" and "legitimate." Without hesitation Paulette indicated that she knew someone with those credentials. She had known Annette Martin since childhood and integrity was certainly a trait Paulette had come to associate with this woman who was also a well-known psychic. I found this assessment echoed by Detective Sergeant Richard Keaton, who has had personal experience using Annette Martin's professional skills in solving serious police investigations. He states,

"Annette Martin has been a consulting psychic with law enforcement agencies across the country for more than 18 years. Her cases have involved local, state, and federal departments. Annette's insight into homicide and missing persons cases has been an outstanding tool for numerous police detectives. Her successes have been many on an endless variety of cases. Psychic investigation should be considered and pursued by law enforcement personnel. Cops routinely respond to anonymous calls. Why not respond to psychics with proven investigative skills?

"Once you have shared these writings, the development of your sixth sense will possibly be unlimited. If you practice what is taught here your rewards could know no bounds."

> Detective Sergeant Richard Keaton
> Marin Sheriff's Department
> Marin County, California

At the start of my first session of *Discovering Your Psychic World*, I brought with me a healthy skepticism grounded in my disciplined training in critical thinking, diagnostic skills, and personality assessment. In my profession a person who speaks about a "sixth sense" may border on having a psychotic disorder. However, Annette did not fit this pattern. As the sessions progressed, my numerous conversations with and observations of Annette interacting with students, proved her to be of sound mind (balanced) and healthy personality.

She has a refreshing enthusiasm that creates an environment of fun and motivates learning. At the same time, careful observation and instruction by Annette set the proper guidelines for using this easily misunderstood ability. This easy-to-understand workbook moves one simply through recognizing and developing one's intuitive skills. It was a delightful surprise as I performed these skills and watched others do likewise. As with any learning experience mistakes are made, but this workbook provides the nonjudgmental encouragement to continue the exercises that accelerate progress.

Indeed, I have found Annette Martin to be a master teacher and look forward to taking her advanced class in this fine series of *Discovering Your Psychic World* . I hope your experiences prove as enjoyable as mine.

Introduction

"Every child that comes into the world is sensitive, but rarely is the child encouraged to recognize and enjoy the benefits of their so-called sixth sense."

Congratulations and welcome to a brand new exciting world. I was lovingly encouraged by my students and husband to assemble this workbook, after 23 years as a professional psychic and 18 years of teaching many thousands of students through my Institute of Intuitive Research and many leading universities across the nation.

Discovering Your Psychic World is a unique workbook offering a practical, simple, step-by-step process that unlocks your psychic potential. It works its magic through a series of psychic exercises and activities that uncover your own natural sixth sense.

The adventure begins by showing you how to perceive your inner light. The master key to this is self-awareness through *creative relaxation*. You will learn to feel a color sent from another's mind and feel the emotions of others. The interpretation of your dreams and an understanding of your own symbols will become clear. You will learn to see auras and practice telepathy and psychometry (reading the vibrations given off by inanimate objects). Dowsing for water or disturbances in the body is another step in your education, with instructions on automatic writing and using a pendulum. You will practice remote viewing and learn to hear sounds that have no physical source. You will say good-bye to stress, predict phone calls and letters, read another person, and gain insight into your own true nature and innate powers of the mind that you never knew existed.

There are numerous exercises, activities, and homework, with solid explanations of how and why the psychic sixth sense works. *Discovering Your Psychic World* has a private psychic diary in which to record experiences and keep track of your growing progress.

Those who have used *Discovering Your Psychic World* have found their lives transformed. The benefits of improving one's psychic potential goes far beyond parlor tricks. Your perceptions of the world will change, creating a more positive and wholesome attitude that will carry you through life.

Students who have used it dramatically improved their concentration and creativity. Psychologists are able to probe more deeply than they previously thought possible. Business executives, through increased confidence in their intuition, are able to make better decisions, forecasts, and personnel choices.

You will begin to understand what others are doing, feeling, and thinking. You will soon know what your future holds. By developing your sixth sense, you will open up entirely new avenues of communication with others, intuit what someone will say next, and respond to what is really going on instead of what appears to be happening. You will begin to learn how to resolve the inner contradictions that produce conflict, and help eliminate the negative beliefs about psychic skills, about yourself, and the world that are holding you back from success. When you discover your psychic world you will open the doorways to self discovery and recovery and allow inner positive healing to happen.

Introduction

Annette Martin

She Who See's With Her Eye's Closed

"At the tender age of seven a wonderful and unusual new world began. While playing with a group of friends, I had a sudden vision in which my playmates would turn on me with intent to kill. Ten minutes later that vision became a reality."

The children chased me into a doorway where they began stoning me, for no reason. A deep baritone voice spoke out, "Pick up that stick." I whirled around thinking that it was Daddy, but there was nothing but the locked wooden door. A horrible pain filled my body and I realized that a large stick had struck the back of my head. Dazed, I turned and faced the angry faces of my friends as the voice spoke again, "Pick up that stick and throw it!" The commanding voice halted my sobs and I looked down. There at my feet lay a gnarly wooden stick about two inches in diameter and a foot long. Instinctively I knew that I had to make an important decision, either to live or die!

The stick went straight out and met its mark across one boy's nose, sending blood gushing everywhere. No sooner had he screamed, than all the front doors flew open and parents came from everywhere, shouting and screaming. My grandmother came to my rescue and took me home. Three days later I had to return and face my pursuers. My best friend Pamela and the others never spoke about that fateful day.

First Medical Diagnosis

Several weeks later, I began to see and experience another mysterious and magical world filled with colorful large pictures that I didn't understand and strange whooshing sounds that lived within people's bodies. When I explained to my family what I was experiencing, they listened and never laughed.

The following week, mother's best friend, Pauline came over for lunch. After she left I said to my parents, "Mommy, Pauline's big right toe really hurts. She needs to go see the doctor." "Pauline didn't say anything about her big toe hurting, Annette, but maybe I will phone her tomorrow," Mother replied.

The next evening the phone rang. It was Pauline. "Vi, you will never believe, but after I left your house, my right big toe began to hurt. I went to the podiatrist and he had to take off the nail. He said I had a very bad infection for a long time."

Musical Career

At fourteen my dramatic flair and singing ability led me into a career with musical comedy and a weekly television show on the Del Courtney Show. By seventeen, I was singing with the Sacramento Music Circus and the San Francisco Civic Light Opera Company. Numerous lead roles in musical comedy and opera followed as my family and I traveled to various assignments around the world. My musical career culminated with *La Boheme* and *Manon Lescout* with the Mexico City National Opera.

Introduction

I was the first North American in twenty-five years allowed to perform with them.

Becoming A Professional Psychic

In 1970 while stepping off a 747 airplane in Hong Kong, I heard these words, "Now Is the Time." Little did I realize that this would be the beginning of a long career as a psychic counselor. My family and I had barely settled in our new home when the phone began to ring, "Can you help me with a problem, Annette? I hear that you do readings and are learning palmistry." I agreed and ended up with the phone ringing off the hook. "Annette, you have to put a stop to this. It is disturbing our home life," my husband announced. "The only way to control the situation would be to charge for my services. and then maybe the phone calls will stop," I said. Wrong! The next day a lady called and said she would be delighted to pay for her reading.

Film on Diagnosing

On December 10, 1975, Dr. G. Jampolsky, psychiatrist, author, speaker, and founder of the Center for Attitudinal Healing and Dr. Jerome Littell, MD., set up an experiment to demonstrate psychic diagnosis. I was escorted into San Rafael High School where I was confronted by a research team of 12 doctors and cameras. One of the patients, introduced as "Laura," was seated at a long table next to the doctors. I was brought into the room and seated opposite Laura and immediately began to scribble words and pictures on my yellow legal pad.

"Something's severed!" I gasped. "It's between the waist and the top of the spine." Tears began to pour down my face. "I don't see any movement. You're paralyzed."

"That's right," Laura nodded.

"I see an automobile hit a wall and I hear a terrible crash" I continued. "It's a car accident and you're pinned inside. That accident left you paralyzed." After verifying that the patient indeed had been paralyzed as a result of a car accident, Dr. Jampolsky suggested that I describe Laura's personality trait's for the doctors.

"She has a lot of tension, a tremendous amount of stress," I began. "Laura's personality is introverted and she's inclined to hold anger within herself." A personality profile that the patient had filled out prior to the experiment matched this description. I continued to point out a hearing problem. Laura nodded, explaining to the doctors that she had once had a mastoid infection.

"It affected your balance, didn't it?" I asked, and then continued without waiting for an answer. "I see you listing to the left."

"Yes, that happened when I was a child," the patient answered. "I couldn't walk without holding on to something because I'd fall to the left side. The infection was in my left ear. I still have some hearing difficulty."

"That was wonderful Annette!" Dr. Jampolsky said. An hour later two other children were seated at the table and I continued to diagnose their conditions. Three hours later, Dr. Jampolsky announced that I had accurately diagnosed all three of the patients physical and emotional states and cause of medical conditions with a 90 percent accuracy. The film made that night has been shown at numerous medical conferences over the years.

Film- Altered States of Consciousness

Hartley Productions produced *Altered States of Consciousness,* a film in which Paul Solomon and I demonstrate medical diagnosis with several patients.

Introduction

A Doctor's Dilemma

Four months later, while Dr. Littell was observing a medical reading for one of Dr. Jampolsky's patients, he asked if I could do a diagnosis on him. I told Dr. Littell that the source of his pain was the upper neck in the region of the second or third vertebra and recommended a chiropractor, a doctor Frank Caldwell in Sausalito.

"Do you know him?" Dr. Littell asked.

"No, I've never heard of him, the name just came to me. I don't even know any chiropractors," I responded.

Dr. Littell stared and explained, "I awoke with an excruciating headache three days ago, which was constant, intense, and post-orbital and inter-temporal in distribution. I have never experienced a headache such as this. Aspirin, codeine, heat, position change had no effect. There has been no let up day or night; it has been almost unbearable, completely incapacitating."

Dr. Littell phoned the next day and announced there was a Dr. Frank Caldwell in Sausalito, and one hour after a cervical adjustment he was completely free of the headache. "Thank you, Annette. You are incredible," he said.

1986 -   Psychic Warns Housewife She Needs Surgery - Hours Before Doctor Confirms It

When Jean S. consulted Campbell psychic Annette Martin for a "psychic reading about her trip to South America," she was shocked to hear that she needed immediate surgery.

"Annette drew a picture of my gall bladder with little round black things inside." The same afternoon, Jean went to see Dr. Richard Gardner, upon Annette's insistence. The doctor took an x-ray, immediately sent her to the hospital and two days later performed a gall bladder operation.

"The psychic was correct in her diagnosis," confirmed Dr. Gardner, a San Francisco surgeon. "I took the gall bladder out and it was full of dark green gallstones that looked black."

15 Year Old Skin Problem

During the summer of 1989, Ezra L. came to see me. He had been afflicted with a painful skin problem for fifteen years, despite two operations, x-ray treatments, and injections. During the reading I gave him a diet to follow.

Dr. Benjamin H. Moore, who treated Ezra, said, "This diet seems to have had a positive effect on what was a serious skin condition. It is cured and you have lost fifty pounds as well. Interesting!"

Honolulu Star Newspaper

Dear Annette,

Many days have passed where my thoughts have sought you out. I am enclosing a copy of the medical certificate. You told me in the reading that I needed a hysterectomy and to please see my gynecologist as soon as possible. I followed your feelings, even though I had no symptoms of problems and made an appointment. As you can see from the certificate you were absolutely right. He operated three weeks later.

Mahalo for being a part of us, you're such a beautiful person.

Aloha, Rosie

Introduction

Dr. Bob Culver - 1990

Dear Annette,

Each of the ten people mentioned below referred to me by you had a positive and dramatic response, indicating to me that you had been accurate in your appraisal of the problem and the probable solution. Thank you so much for your continued support, you are great. Bob Culver, D. C. Foothill Chiropractic.

Cosmopolitan Magazine - 1991
"Police Use Psychic Annette Martin to Help Solve 35-Year-Old Double Murder"

Cosmopolitan magazine featured an article on many different law enforcement cases that Annette helped solve that led to a guest appearance on the *Montel Williams Show.*

Carolyn Mc Cormick - 1994   Market Manager - Anthony Robbins

"Annette Martin's insight is both gifted and accurate. She gave me insight on how to open-up the relationship with my 21 year old son. I followed her guidance and as a result: we are once again best friends and it seemed to occur without conversation or effort. When you hear her information, your heart sings for it feels the truth of her wisdom."

My Dream

One of my dreams has been to educate and bring forward the awareness of our incredible mind, in a form that is fun and easy to understand. In 1983, a more scientific investigation of my talents was made by Jeffrey Mishlov, Ph.D. in his book *PSI, Development Systems* published by Ballantine Books. I knew at that point, it was time to start putting my notes together.

My professional work has included assisting police departments throughout the nation: the FBI; the Marin County, California, Sheriffs Department; the Reno, Nevada, Task Force for Missing Children; the Cascade County, Montana, Sheriff's Department; the Martinez, California, Police Department, and many more. I worked primarily on murder investigations and child abduction cases. Privately, I counsel individuals and many companies, including Lockheed, Sun Microsystems, Hughes Aircraft, and dozens of smaller firms.

The term "Radio Psychic" has been labeled to my name because of my numerous radio shows for the past 15 years. Currently I can be heard on KEST, KNRY, K108, KGLO 1450am in Northern California, and formerly co-hosted a daily morning talk show at KGU in Honolulu, Hawaii, with Hollywood announcer Don La Mond.

I have been a featured speaker at conferences in many other states and Canadian provinces and many foreign countries, including Hong Kong. I have lectured at the famed Psychological Studies Institute in Palo Alto, California, and the Parapsychology Institute in New York.

Jennifer Green, well known artist has included me in a painting titled "Mandala-Healing Universe" with Native American and international Shaman. It has been shown in art galleries and New Mexico state buildings.

Introduction

How To Use This Book

As we go through ***Discovering Your Psychic World,*** I will use my experiences to show how these techniques work. The adventure begins by showing you how to perceive your inner light. The master key is self awareness through creative relaxation. You will learn to feel the emotions of others, practice telepathy and psychometry (reading the vibrations given off by inanimate objects), see auras, analyze and interpret dreams and gain insight into your own true nature and your innate powers of the mind you never knew existed.

There are numerous exercises, activities, and skill enhancing homework, with solid explanations of how and why the psychic, sixth sense works. You will be surprised, with a little time and effort, how soon you will be using these new found skills.

Each chapter begins with background material to orient you to the subject. Self assessment tools enable you to define and evaluate your position regarding the topic. Throughout the book you will find clear and concise exercises and meditations with worksheets to fill out on your progress. By practicing each exercise you will teach your self to develop and enhance your sixth sense. All chapters include a homework schedule.

Do not drink any alcoholic beverage four hours or less before each class or chapter. The alcohol will dull your senses and your ability to do the exercises. Do not use drugs, such as antibiotics during your practice sessions as they will dull the very mental abilities you are now in the process of developing.

It is recommended that you take each chapter at a time and start at the beginning. **Do not practice the exercises longer than specified. Do not push yourself, thinking that longer is better**. This is the format that I have been using for the past 18 years of teaching and have found it to work miracles if used in sequence. If you jump around throughout the book you will find yourself confused and not understanding the process of developing your sixth sense.

Remember to keep an open mind and work on mastering each skill before going on to the next exercise. It is impossible to learn how to dance unless you practice. Always be positive in your attitude and use of your new-found skills.

We have also produced an audio companion set, ***Peaceful White Light meditation*** tapes. They comprise the first six meditations in this book. We have used the music from my dear friend Steven Halpern. People from four to 80 years old are using these tapes for bedtime relaxation and stress reduction. For more information on tapes turn to page 161.

Above all, have fun, be patient with yourself and......................

May The White Light Be With You,

Annette Martin

Chapter 1

Taking Inventory

Before we begin our journey, we must take an inventory of ourselves and find out where we are in our development. There are many different directions we can follow to grow in consciousness. It is most important to set an ideal. Let us begin with a self analysis.

Answer each question and score the correct number

1 = Never or rarely happens.

2 = Occasionally occurs.

3 = Frequently happens.

Enter Score

_____ 1. How often do you experience a strong hunch or feeling on what you should or should not do?

_____ 2. Suddenly you thought of someone whom you have not thought of in months or years and you get a letter or phone call from that person?

_____ 3. Have you received impressions about people when you were talking to them or just thinking about them?

_____ 4. If someone asks you what you think about an other person are you absolutely correct in what you felt or sensed?

_____ 5. Have you ever had a premonition that something was going to happen and it did?

_____ 6. When making a decision you ask advice of family or friends and they give it. You know deep inside that they are wrong but you follow it anyway?

_____ 7. Do you have dreams that later come true?

_____ 8. Have you noticed unusual coincidences in your life or things that you have read or heard about?

_____ 9. Do you often awaken with an answer or solution to a problem that was on your mind when you went to sleep?

_____ 10. Have you ever thought you saw an apparition or a ghost-like form of someone living or passed away?

_____ 11. Have you ever had the sensation of leaving your body and visiting a distant place?

Taking Inventory

_____ 12. Have you ever thought you heard a voice of a departed loved one warning or giving assurances to you?

_____ 13. Have you known what was inside an unopened present to you?

_____ 14. Do you have dreams about other people and find out that what you saw in your dreams was true?

_____ 15. Do you find your dreams telling you things that are coming up in the future or perhaps clearing things up in the past?

_____ 16. Do you sometimes get an urge to go into a particular shop because you know that you will find what you are looking for?

_____ 17. How often do you get a gut feeling about someone or a situation that proves to be accurate?

_____ 18. How often in the early morning, just before waking, do you get impressions or novel ideas about situations in the world or in your life?

_____ 19. How often do you daydream?

_____ 20. Do you get feelings of "deja vu," the feeling that you have been through this experience before?

_____ 21. When someone has lost something, do you get strong impressions of where to look and they turn out to be correct?

_____ 22. How often do you get a strong sense of knowing what is going to happen next?

_____ 23. How often have you sensed danger around the corner?

_____ 24. How frequently have you sensed a loved one in trouble, either near or far away?

_____ ADD UP YOUR TOTAL

Your score will give you an idea of how intuitive you are right now. We will be working on improving your intuitive skills as we move through the exercises in this course.

Your Score	
72	Highly intuitive
51 - 71	Intuitive
20 - 50	Average

Chapter 2

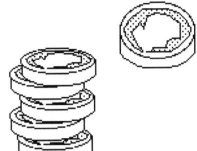

ESP -
The Sixth Sense

If any of these experiences have happened to you, it is possible that you had a manifestation of what is today called intuition, extra sensory perception or ESP.

Extra-sensory perception has long been assumed to be an almost magical ability, one belonging more to the world of myth and fairy than to everyday reality. Many scientist, whose forebears waged a long battle against ignorance and superstition in the eighteenth and nineteenth centuries, are angry and hostile to the very idea of ESP, or who, prefer to ignore it's existence, despite the positive results obtained by those few who have experimentally investigated it.

Support for the possibility of ESP comes from the discoveries of quantum physicists, who work at the cutting edge of science. They have introduced such concepts as relativity, action-at-a-distance, anti-matter, black holes and parallel universes to both their colleagues and to the general public.

A Dr. J. B. Rhine made this term familiar in the United States in 1937 when he published his monograph, *Extrasensory Perception*. In 1940 he published *Extrasensory Perception after Sixty Years*. The term caught on and soon became a household word. He interpreted it to mean *perception of those things and phenomena that reside beyond or outside the ordinary senses.*

Dr. Rhine adopted the term from Dr. Rudolf Tischner, an ophthalmologist from Munich in the 1920s who also conducted research into psychical and occult phenomena. Tischner used the term to explain "externalization of sensibility," which goes back to 1892, when the French researcher Dr. Paul Joire first used ESP to describe the phenomenon of an individual's ability to sense something outside the body without the use of any known physical senses.

One of the epochal studies of the overall psychic experience was published in 1923 by Dr. Eugene Osty, director of the Institute Metaphysique International in Paris. The book was titled *La Connaissance Supranormale*. He establishes that humans possess some sensing mechanisms that "go out" and connect on a supernormal level with information that "comes in."

Russian Scientists

Russian scientists use the term bioinformation, rather than extrasensory perception to describe phenomena such as clairvoyance, precognition, telepathy, and ESP. Bioinformation focuses the individual's attention on getting "information" rather than upon some hypothetical faculty that might be implied by ESP.

I agree with Dr. Osty and the Russian scientists. From my personal experiences, of being a psychic child and extensive research as a professional for the past 25 years, I feel that these manifestations are not coming from an *extra sense,* but instead are from our *sixth sense,* or what I like to call, *the survival sense,* which lies within the right or creative side of the brain and houses the subconscious, unconscious mind.

ESP - The Sixth Sense

We are all born with six senses, although in our society we only declare and cultivate our five senses of hearing, seeing, smelling, tasting, and feeling. Our environment and behavioral patterns dictate how we will develop all these senses.

So then we can claim that *We all are psychic!* I do believe that the sixth sense or survival sense that we all have is very natural.

Scholars and scientists today are studying ESP or the sixth sense and are beginning to agree that everyone has the capacity to be intuitive to a degree. By developing, educating, and practicing, the skill can be acquired.

Are We Asleep to Our Surroundings?

Is it possible that we as a species are suffering from a collective amnesia? Perhaps, as Homo Sapiens, we have forgotten something that our ancestors once knew and practiced daily. They had a certain type of perception and attitude. Man could understand and identify with non-human life, had a great respect for the unexplained, and felt a deep humbleness for the complexities of their world.

What is happening today?

What generally occurs is that this sixth sense or feeling is squashed either by family, friends or teachers. It is very difficult being the oddball, such as telling people to be careful because you have a feeling something is going to happen to them. The child would probably get into trouble and be told not to say such things or respond in such a sensitive manner to situations.

Johnny is not supposed to cry, goes the story. Johnny is not supposed to feel what he is feeling, so he learns not to feel. We stop this very natural part of our being with our children. We are supposed to fit into the mold of everyone else and keep quiet, be like Susie or Ralph. Don't show your feelings.

You might have had a spontaneous psychic experience unexpectedly and did not know how to interpret it correctly. It could have been very distressing, but as you develop your sixth sense and arouse the dormant aspects of your consciousness, you are likely to have many unfamiliar experiences. We are going to learn to be prepared, so you can learn to enjoy and appreciate your new world as well as feel assured to counsel others when their psychic faculties open up unexpectedly.

As we observe the world today, it is slowly changing, but we still have a long way to go. The human lived by his sixth sense or survival sense, for many centuries. He did this by knowing and feeling inside himself that danger lurked, nearby. The men knew where the game was, they could smell the scent of the animal, track it down, and feed their families. Ancient man could tell where water was located by using all of his senses.

Feeling Nature

I will never forget one morning on safari in Africa. We were looking for lions but none were to be found. The Serengehti was littered with every other animal, rhinoceros, zebra, elephants, giraffe, and monkeys, but no lions.

ESP - The Sixth Sense

We had traveled five miles further and suddenly the driver stopped our jeep. Our guide told us to be very quiet. The four of us strained our eyes to see, but there was nothing but brown dirt, scrub brush, and a few trees.

Within five minutes of utter silence, a lioness emerged out of nowhere. She totally ignored us and strutted in front of our jeep. We watched as she strode across the desert, knowing that she was in full control of the situation. I don't think any of us had taken a breath for the entire time. After she was out of sight, I asked our guide, "Did you see her in the distance? He turned and smiled, "No, I didn't see her, Mamsab, but I could feel her." I nodded my head and replied, "Yes."

But I ask you, do we need to "survive," currently? Very few of us have to do that right now. To sum it up, we have lost the *skill* of using our sixth sense or survival sense, because we just don't need it, so we think. It is so easy to retrieve that part of ourselves, if we want to. But it is most definitely in the wanting**!**

Are Women More in Touch Than Men with Their Sixth Sense ?

Scientists feel that women probably have a biological advantage in this department. In the female brain there is a larger network of fibers linking the right and left hemispheres. This can allow a faster response time between the right and left brain. So this gives the female a head start on combining logic and her sixth sense. The female also uses a magnetic sense which is connected to her menstrual cycle and the phases of the moon.

Also the limbic system of the female works differently, which keeps her in close touch with her off-spring. Women will tend to feel their flashes of ESP or sixth sense differently than males. A female may feel a tightening in the diaphragm or stomach, when she knows for sure that she is receiving information.

I began doing this at a very young age and couldn't understand why I was always having stomach aches.

Men feel their flashes of intuition differently, most often by a sensation of warmth in the chest area. They are what we call electrically based versus magnetic. Males will tend to use their sixth sense for problem solving.

ESP - The Sixth Sense

Left Brain Connection to the Right Brain

LEFT
- Language
- Mathematics
- Reasoning
- Physical World
- Science
- Logic

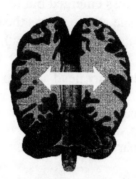

RIGHT
- Intuition
- Art
- Creativity
- Imagination
- Insight

By a process of relaxation and exercises, you will be learning how to connect this network of fibers linking your left brain to your right brain. When we are receiving insight or a flash through our sixth sense, we are creating an arc of energy that reaches over from the right brain to the left brain. It is then processed into either a feeling, picture, odors, taste, or just a "knowing." The sides of our brain control the opposite sides of the body.

We all have the capacity to learn how to develop this skill. I do not feel that being aware of our sixth sense is supernatural, beyond our comprehension, or devil worship.

Can I Tune into My Body and Mind?

If you want to know what is wrong with your body, you can tune into the body and ask it, the answer will come to you. You do know this information, you know everything about yourself.

You can do the same with your mind. You only have to allow yourself to let it be there. You really don't need a psychic, astrologer, or numerologist to tell you about yourself. They are only acting as a mirror for you. You will begin to understand yourself in a new and different way.

Understanding Who You Are Can Help You

How you think basically determines not only what sixth you are but how you are, how others react to you, how you react to them, and what constitutes the real values in life and living. Don't you think it

ESP - The Sixth Sense

is time to devote a few minutes a day to the business of getting in touch with your own mind so that you can learn to operate it more efficiently?

We think in mental pictures and not in words! Everything that happens to us takes the form of a mental picture in your memory. Recorded with it is the feeling or emotional reaction you had at the time. Perhaps you had an aroused feeling of hate or fear, these impressions have now become a part of your subconscious mind.

We all have had the experience of discovering and saying, "What is the name of that mutual friend of ours? I can't quite remember it." Then the next morning I'll remember it. You've had that same experience. So we all have the experience of asking ourselves a question that gets answered by ourselves later on. In other words, this tells us we have a reliable subconscious functioning operative in our brains even while we sleep.

Even if an event happened in the past, it is still having an effect upon you. All of your experiences, up to the present moment, are still alive in another form in your memory stream. If this were not true, then you could not recall them at will or be mentally or emotionally disturbed upon remembering an unhappy situation, or fear the recurrence of some tragic or regretted circumstance.

You are influenced not only by how you reacted, mentally and emotionally, to past experiences, but by the nature of your desires and aspirations as well as your fears and hates. Your subconscious mind is designed to reproduce for you, in your outer life, whatever you picture.

Remember that the subconscious mind has no capacity for reasoning. It merely follows along what the conscious mind has dictated, accepting all feelings and associated mental pictures, as though they were blueprints to be reproduced in your outer world. Your conscious mind, with the exercise of your reason and your will, represents the only force that can change or eliminate these pictures that the subconscious mind is holding.

If you keep telling your subconscious mind that it is impossible for it to transcend space and time, then you will never be able to experience ESP. You must remember that your subconscious mind cannot reason. I must repeat it only can follow your direction issued by your conscious mind.

What happens when ESP comes in?

Suddenly you may find mental pictures and strong feelings from the minds of others fleeting in and out of your consciousness, or even taking temporary possession. You may not understand what is happening and interpret these impressions as coincidences or happenstance. At other times the ESP experience will be so vivid and unmistakably true that you will know something beyond the ordinary has happened, even though you cannot explain it.

You may experience physical sensations around the head area, such as a tingling of the scalp, a tickling sensation on the face, a feeling of pressure around the top of the head, or a sense of energy coming directly through the frontal lobe. These physical sensations will emanate from the portions of the brain which are aroused to new levels of consciousness. These physical sensations can be used as a signal that you are receiving information. Others may feel a pulling in the stomach area, the hands or face flushing and in my case, "goose-bumps."

Bucky

"Intuition Often Turns Dreams Into Demonstrable Facts "

R. Buckminster Fuller   March, 1983

It was the summer of 1982 when I had the honor of meeting one of the greatest minds of our time, R. Buckminster Fuller, futurist, philosopher, scientist, author, architect, cosmologist. Bucky, as he preferred to be called, spoke on how we needed to take care of Mother Earth, at a conference being held at the Highland Hospital on the beautiful island of Maui.

During a cocktail party held later that evening, I turned to notice Bucky motioning me over. My heart raced and couldn't believe that he wanted to speak to me. I turned, thinking that he must be communicating with someone behind my back, but no one else was standing there. I pointed to myself and he nodded his head. Walking over to his table of five I thought to myself, "What will I say to this extraordinary man?"

Within seconds I found myself sitting next to this incredible mind, tongue tied for the first time in my life. Bucky smiled and asked my name and then said, "Tell me, Annette, who you are."

"Oh, my God! Who I am?" I thought to myself. Looking into this octogenarians bright blue sparkling eyes and knowing deep in my heart that I had to speak the truth, I stammered, "I am a professional Psychic."

"Yes, yes!" he replied. "Now, tell me all about yourself. Start from the beginning and tell me everything." He took my right hand and held it gently. "Speak loudly so I can hear, this is my good ear, so we shouldn't have to much trouble."

Before I knew it an hour and a half had passed and I was being invited to dinner with Buckminster Fuller, an astronaut who flew to the moon, and two other physicist. I couldn't believe what was happening.

Bucky took my hand and said, "Annette, I want you to sit on my left, so we can talk during dinner and you can tell us how you are able to read other people."

I began to explain my process and would get to a certain point, when Bucky would interrupt and explain to the other's in scientific terms what I had just said. They would all discuss the issue and ask me to go on. By the time we finished desert I was exhausted from trying to comprehend some of the technical terminology Bucky had been using. Everyone was smiling and seemed to be having a good time, so I presumed they understood.

ESP - The Sixth Sense

We drove back to the Hotel and stepped out of the car. I thanked them for the lovely dinner when Bucky leaned over and hugged me. He took both of my hands and put them up to his face. "Annette, I want you to promise me one thing," he said gently. "Promise me that you will always continue with your work in the psychic field, your readings, teaching and what ever form it takes."

Tears streamed down my face as our eyes met, "Oh, yes, Bucky, I will always continue, till my dying day. I promise you."

"Good! Now, I hope to see you sometime soon," he said shaking my hands.

I stood there in a daze as he walked off with the others.

Several months later I was fortunate to be able to attend Bucky's world-map conference game in San Diego, which led to three other visits throughout the United States. Each time we would sit and talk about his philosophy and he would want to always know what I had learned since we last met.

One of the issues that we spoke about in great detail was the belief we both have that human continuance depends entirely upon:

- The intuitive wisdom of each and every individual.

- The individual's integrity of speaking and acting only on the individual's own within-self-intuited and reasoned initiative.

- The individual's comprehensive informedness.

- The individual's joining action with others, as motivated only by the individually conceived consequences of so doing.

- The individual's never-joining action with others, created by emotionalism, or by a sense of the crowd's power to overwhelm, or fear of holding to a course by one's own intellectual convictions.

It was a sad day when I heard the news that my wonderful old friend Bucky had passed away two hours before his wife Annie died. In my heart I feel he knew intuitively that she would be lost without him. I am sure he planned it this way so that he would be there to hold her hand and walk through the light together.

This great man has made such a mark on my soul and continues to give me a propulsion of energy to continue on.

ESP - The Sixth Sense

I will have more to say about the mind as we move along, but for now I would like you to fill in the following questionnaire.

What do you expect to learn from this workbook?

_____

_____

_____

_____

_____

_____

_____

_____

_____

_____

Write a few sentences about an unhappy event in your life.

_____

_____

_____

_____

_____

_____

_____

_____

_____

_____

_____

Chapter 3

Keys to Understanding
Your Sixth Sense

Love Yourself
I believe the main moving force that activates our psychic ability or sixth sense, is love of self. We must *love ourselves* unselfishly. If we want love in our life, than we must be loving. Parents, children, and close friends have experiences of the sixth sense, especially in times of danger, because of love. This emotion of love is so powerful that it transcends time and space and transmits itself to those we love. Learn to accept and love yourself for who you are.

Forgive Yourself
Don't knock yourself down or punish yourself for past deeds. Stop condemning yourself and *forgive yourself*. List the good things you have done in your life at the end of this chapter. Once you understand this, you will begin to see the good in others.

Change Your Attitude
An attitude that will be most helpful in advancing your psychic development, will be *enthusiasm* for the self-studies and work involved. You have taken the first step in that direction by getting this workbook.

Trust

Many people talk about incidents when they had an intuitive hunch and unfortunately failed to follow through with it. This *lack of trust* can be a stumbling block for you. When we are learning to skate or ride a bicycle we must fall a few times to learn how to balance our bodies. We must be willing to trust our new found psychic or sixth sense ability, even if it means making a few mistakes in the beginning. We must listen to those intuitive flashes so that we can learn to develop and use them in our everyday living.

Be Alert
Have you noticed that when you get frightened all of your senses are heightened and you become keenly aware of what is going on around you? Your body, mind, and soul go into "Alert." This state of *alertness* is one of the keys to understanding how you can activate your sixth sense.

Want to Help Others
There needs to be a sense of *wanting to give to others*. You need to have a feeling of sharing information. If there is a need to covet or hold back what you know or feel you will never be able to communicate to others.

Keys to Understanding

Have a Good Sense of Humor

If there is a *good sense of humor*, you can receive and give information much more easily. The understanding of the psychic information will be more palatable and you can assimilate it more fully.

Exercise

Exercise is beneficial in keeping the body in good physical condition and can help make your sensory system more attuned and alert. It creates a balance on the endocrine glands and helps to open our spiritual centers.

Write a short description of how you feel about each of these keys.

1. Love Yourself

_____
_____
_____
_____
_____
_____

2. Forgive Yourself

_____
_____
_____
_____
_____
_____
_____

3. Change Your Attitude

_____
_____
_____
_____
_____
_____

Keys to Understanding

4. Trust

_____

_____

_____

_____

_____

_____

5. Be Alert

_____

_____

_____

_____

_____

_____

6. Want to Assist Others

_____

_____

_____

_____

_____

_____

7. Have a Good Sense of Humor

_____

_____

_____

_____

_____

_____

8. Exercise

_____

_____

_____

_____

Keys to Understanding

Make a list of good things you have done in your life.

_____

_____

_____

_____

_____

_____

_____

_____

_____

_____

_____

_____

_____

_____

_____

_____

_____

_____

_____

_____

_____

_____

_____

_____

_____

_____

_____

_____

Keys to Understanding

Confidence

I would like to address one more aspect of ourselves, before we go on.

Confidence! Confidence in my book means that you have the ability to be comfortable with yourself, whether you are right or wrong, whether you need to go ahead with something or let it go. Whatever has to be done or understood can be done with assurance and without self - judgment.

Our judgment has a tendency to undermine our confidence. When we begin to judge ourselves as being success or failures when circumstances and situations around us succeed or fail, we lost confidence. What we do then is hide or shield ourselves from what we would consider failures, or mistakes. We need to bolster up our successes. What happens is that we stop seeing ourselves as complete and whole, and we have begun to block off our ability to listen and pay attention to our intuition when it says something we find difficult to accept.

We need to feel comfortable with ourselves and that means all of ourselves, fat legs, big hips, no breast, losing our hair: mistakes and successes we have made in the past.

You need to feel free and neutral to allow the intuition to flow through you. Do not try, do not be attached to old ways of thinking. With this type of attitude we can focus on how we can change to improve ourselves.

Write about your confidence level

_____
_____
_____
_____
_____
_____
_____
_____
_____
_____
_____
_____
_____
_____
_____
_____
_____
_____

Chapter 4

Meditation - The Master Key

Master Key to your psychic world

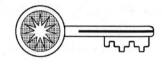

Meditation has been practiced for some 4000 years and perhaps even longer. The master key that will unlock the door to your psychic world lies in *meditation.*

The West and Meditation

We began to participate in objective scientific research in the West around the beginning of the twentieth century. During the 1960's initial experiments were done on the yogis because of their spectacular physiological feats. The yogis had learned to alter their body temperature and heart rate. Scientist found their claims to be valid prompting more investigation.

When I was a young girl attending a Catholic school, I spent a great deal of time praying in church. I had always pointed my prayers to God because my daddy had taught me, "Always go to the top, Honey, when you want something done." Naturally, being a good girl, I listened and did just that. I would ask God questions and then wait for an answer. The answers always came, but often there were no questions.

I would sit in church, take a few deep breaths, close my eyes, and just relax. As time went on, I found that pictures about my family and friends crossed my mind. It was wonderful because I hadn't asked and the pictures were so helpful to what was going on in my life. This continued until I was 18 years old, when someone told me that something other than praying was occurring. I was meditating!

After months of research I discovered that I was beginning an altered state of consciousness-another term for meditation or a self-hypnotic state.

How Can We Train Our Chattering Mind?

Meditation involves switching off your everyday consciousness as far as possible and tuning into your feeling intuitive self. We can train our conscious mind, the left brain, to be still through certain processes to allow ourselves to be in touch with our subconscious, the right brain. This subconscious mind knows everything about us-our past, present, and future.

By quieting the conscious mind we can learn to understand our subconscious. The conscious mind is constantly chattering away. Sometimes it is so noisy that we can't hear or understand what our subconscious is trying to tell us.

Meterdition - The Master Key

All too often we may experience a signal through another part of our body telling us that something is wrong, but we don't always pay attention to the signal. The signal could be a feeling, a picture, our ears ringing, or a sense of smell. Some people call it their gut feeling.

While we are meditating, we are relaxing our bodies and our conscious mind to then allow the subconscious mind to become active. In this part of our mind lies our creative self, or sixth sense.

Physical Benefits of Meditation

Through testing they agreed that the cardiovascular system is clearly affected. Our heart rate drops and with regular practice, blood pressure also falls. Meditation can therefore be useful in treating mild high blood pressure but the benefits dissipate if practice is stopped. Certain meditators can increase the blood flow to the body, thus raising the temperature of fingers and toes. The Tibetan Tumo masters who specialize in this are reported to demonstrate their mastery by meditating semi-naked in the snows of the Tibetan winter.

Blood chemistry can shift and the hormone levels may be modified, lactate levels-sometimes regarded as a measure of relaxation-may fall, and cholesterol may be reduced. (Murphy & Donovan, 1988; Shapiro & Walsh, 1984)

During most meditative practices the EEG slows and more synchronous alpha waves (8 - 13 cycles per second) increase in amount and amplitude. Some TM meditators believe that this can provide a basis for enhanced creativity and psychological growth (Alexander et al., 1991).

Studies have shown that regular meditators have fewer absences from work due to illness. Many stress workshops, books, and videos are selling a form of meditation or relaxation techniques. They have combined them with visualization exercises to relieve anxiety, stress, heart palpitations, and many other related diseases.

Research has found that our mental attitude has a direct bearing on our immune system. We must understand that what we think is what we become.

By spending more time in this part of our brain we can learn more about *who we are, where we have been, and where we are going.* Meditation is simple, but not easy. We need to learn how to discipline the conscious mind.

You may not have experienced this before, but be patient with yourself. My suggestion is to set aside a specific time each day to shut out the distractions of our everyday life. By doing this we may enter within the wonderment of our subconscious mind. Begin with five minutes and work up to 15 or 20 minutes a day.

We all have this information. What is necessary is for us to look within.

Before we begin to meditate there are three things we need to learn about:

- *White Light*
- **Visualization**
- **Breath.**

Meditation - The Master Key

My first recollection of the *White Light* began at the tender age of nine. One warm September evening while getting ready for bed, I saw a flash. I turned and on the wall directly across from my bed was the face of Jesus. My body froze in shock as I stared transfixed at this sweet, loving face. The illumination around his head was a brilliant, white, clear light. He didn't say anything and before I knew it, the face disappeared. Climbing into bed I said aloud, "Oh, this must be a sign. I wonder if I am supposed to be a nun!"

With that feeling followed many years of going to church every day and looking for the answer. The *White Light* was more present around me as time went on. I could feel the light as the warmth surrounded my body.

After a year or so, I could only see this brilliant *White Light* when I closed my eyes to pray. It was wonderful and comforting. The messages I received always came in the *White Light*, as they still do today.

What Is *White Light* ?

The *White Light* is you, the universe, and God. We can draw this light to us by visualizing it in a form until it becomes a part of our being. The *White Light* is pure, positive loving energy. *We are that energy! We are that God!* We are made in the image and likeness of God. So we are the *White Light* ! We have just lost temporary sight of it, that is all.

What Does It Do for Us?

We can become children of the *White Light* by directing it through our physical, emotional, and mental bodies to circumstances outside ourselves. As we direct more *White Light*, the clearer our vision becomes-of that which is clear and unclear first in ourselves and then in others. The more we use the *White Light*, the greater our awareness, and our sensitivity to the environment around us become.

Our thoughts and actions have a direct relationship upon those within our Circle of Consciousness. Their thoughts and actions affect our consciousness as well. Others are no longer separate from us, but now are a part of us. Disciplining yourself will enable your consciousness to affect your environment, lest your environment affect your consciousness.

How Do We Use It?

Not only will you become a being of *White Light*, but you can use this to communicate telepathically throughout the universe, dimensions, and time. As your awareness grows and the ability to use the *White Light* increases, you will find yourself traveling instantly, via the *White Light*, throughout worlds unknown to you before, meeting new friends and old ones of times long past. You will realize that there is no separation in time, only our lack of awareness of the *White Light*.

Meditation - The Master Key

The more awareness of the *White Light*, the better you can focus your consciousness. If you focus without attachment, this will allow the *White Light* to work more quickly and effectively.

You may focus the *White Light* on your car to protect it from harm. Wrap your home in the light, protecting it from invaders. Circle it around your loved ones. You can direct the *White Light* to anything or anyone you wish to protect with positive energy. The more you use the light, with focused attention, the stronger and easier it will be to direct it to your subject. You will truly become a child of *White Light*.

We will be using the *White Light* each time we begin our meditations and practice our exercises. I cannot emphasize enough how important it is to use this tool which is free.

Guided Visualizations

In the not-too-distant future, mental videos may be a prescription for a headache, cold, virus, weight loss, or chronic pain. They could be called "creative imagery" or "visualizations" that conjure vivid pictures in the mind. It's been my experience, as well as that of thousands of students who have crossed my portals, that visualization can influence our health and well-being indirectly-and sometimes powerfully.

There is a tremendous amount of research going on in the scientific community suggesting that visualizing certain pictures may help us fight disease-or make it easier to endure-by reducing stress and promoting relaxation, as well as influencing the immune system for the better. Numerous doctors and hospitals are combining visualization with traditional therapy, as we have seen in the eye-opening PBS television program with Bill Moyers, "Healing and the Mind."

I feel that creative visualizations can be one of the most important tools we have for creating and maintaining good health. A basic principle in holistic health is that we cannot separate our physical health from our emotional, mental, and spiritual states of being. As I explain to my clients, all three states are connected and a state of "dis-ease" in the body is most often a reflection of conflict, tension, anxiety or dis- harmony on other levels of being as well. When we have a physical disorder, it is important to look within at our emotional and intuitive feelings, to see what we can do to restore harmony and balance. We must learn to tune in and listen to our inner voice.

Creative visualization refers to the way in which we communicate from our mind to our body. It is the process of forming images and thoughts in our mind, consciously or unconsciously, and then transmitting them to the body as signals or commands. By using creative imagery or visualizations, you will learn to focus your awareness on soothing sensations and a passive attitude. Your mind will then naturally grow quiet.

See It, Then Do It

Imaging for success has been popular for years with Olympic athletes and high-powered business executives, people committed to securing every possible advantage for success. And studies prove that it works: What people are able to *see*, they're more likely to be able to do.

In a recent study, college students who were preparing for public speaking significantly reduced their apprehension using visualizations. They were asked to envision the best possible scenario: putting on just the right clothes; feeling clear, confident and thoroughly prepared; giving a smooth, brilliant speech that was well received. If imagining a positive outcome promotes success on the playing field or at the podium, is it possible that thinking healthy thoughts might lead to better health? It's only a theory at this point, but some physicians believe it's a distinct possibility.

Meditation - The Master Key

Tapping Your Inner Wisdom

Clinicians at the Behavioral Medicine clinic in San Diego, California integrate imagery into treatment, using it both to elicit the relaxation response and for the reduction of chronic pain.

The mechanisms for registering pain in the body are very complex. One natural human response to pain is to tense around it to protect the area. And when you tighten one place, you tighten others. You end up suffering a lot of secondary pain and tension in addition to the initial pain. That begins a vicious circle of pain and tension. To break the cycle, patients can identify the physical and emotional tensions that perpetuate it.

Imaging pictures or symbols of what their pain looks like often offers patients the clues needed to help break the cycle. Under the guidance of the skilled professional, creative imaging exercises combined with talking with the patient to help clarify the nature of the pain, by showing where and how tension is being held in the body. This, in turn, often helps them reduce the pain by giving them a better awareness of how it works. Without awareness you don't have the control that allows change.

For instance, finding a clear image of her migraine pain had a dramatic effect on the life of a woman who'd suffered frequent hospitalization from headaches for over 25 years. "I'd always had the sense that my pain was like a ball in my head," she says. "And when the ball titled, I knew a doozy was coming. I had no idea, however, that I could control the ball." After this realization, she was able to dramatically reduce the number and severity of her headaches. As soon as she'd feel the ball beginning to tilt, she'd lie down, close her eyes and, through her imagination, take the ball out of head.

The ball symbolized the muscle tension in the neck and head. By making the visual association, the woman was able to release the tension by getting rid of the ball. The easiest way to understand imagery is to experience it for yourself. Like tasting a hot fudge sundae, one bite of the real thing means more than anything anyone could tell you.

The Breath

As the newborn emerges from the womb it begins its path of breath upon the Earth. When observing a young child, you will notice that as each breath is drawn in, the belly goes out and is distended. Upon the exhalation of the breath, the belly goes down. This is what we call the natural breath.

But what happens to us? As we grow, somehow or another, we begin to breathe less and less with the belly and gradually move it up to the chest cavity. This creates a shallow, shorter breath. I ask myself at times if this is because we choose not to experience all that surrounds us.

Have you noticed that when you are despondent or having trouble making a decision you will take a very deep breath, what we call a sigh? What happens when we sigh deeply? We begin to send more oxygen through the cardiovascular system which in turn shoots more blood and oxygen to the brain to relieve stress and tension, thus making us feel far more comfortable.

According to Yoga teaching, Prana-Breath, can be stored in the body and then directed to the mind to different parts, with revitalizing effects. An advanced yogi can live on Prana (breath) instead of food. He appears to know how to replenish the cells of his body through his breathing. The yogic breath is a complete breath in which every part of the lung is filled with air. It increases the intake of oxygen and also Prana. For most people, however, the most that can be achieved is a heightened feeling of well-being and an improvement in health and vitality.

Meditation - The Master Key

Inhaling

Breathing through the nostril is more natural and healthy. Mouth breathing makes you more susceptible to diseases. Between the mouth and lungs, there is nothing to strain the air. Dust, dirt and other impure substances have a clear track to the lungs. Mouth breathing also admits cold air to the lungs, which can lead to inflammation of the respiratory organs.

Nostril breathing is more vitalizing and healthy to your entire energy system. The nostrils and nasal passages are designed with hair to filter and sieve the air. They also warm the air through the mucous membranes. This makes the air fit for the delicate organs of the lungs.

As you inhale through your nose only, you push out the stomach. This movement causes the diaphragm to descend and the lower part of the lungs to be filled. By lifting and expanding the upper ribs the middle part is filled. Expanding the chest further fills the top of the lungs. This is all done in one smooth, continuous movement, without any jerking or raising of the shoulders. The shoulders should stay relaxed and down.

Exhaling

As you exhale, through the mouth only, the stomach is drawn in. This lifts the diaphragm, the ribs return to their normal position and the air expels from the lungs. With this picture in mind you can see why the abdomen is so important in yoga breathing.

Let's Practice Rhythmical Breathing

Put your hands on the abdomen, with fingertips touching, and inhale through the nose, count to six, then exhale through the mouth, counting to six. This slow rhythm of about five breaths to the minute, instead of the usual 15 to 20, is the yoga tempo of deep breathing.

Never inhale through the mouth.

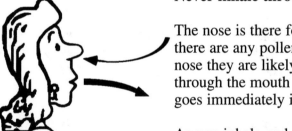

The nose is there for a reason. I see it as the body's vacuum cleaner. If there are any pollens or particles in the air and we breathe in through our nose they are likely to be caught in the hairs of the nose. If you breathe in through the mouth you are constantly picking up particles of debris that goes immediately into the lungs.

As you inhale and exhale you will notice how your fingertips move apart and come together again, demonstrating the expansion and contraction of the stomach. You will experience a feeling of great relaxation and a sense of floating. If possible, devote at least three to five minutes to this deep breathing every day. I suggest in the morning, around 3:00 p.m. and at night before going to sleep.

This can be done any time, when you are feeling down or out of energy. You can do it anywhere — standing, sitting, lying down, whatever. Just close your palms and take the three deep breaths with the light. It will always make you feel better. It is especially helpful if you are frustrated or angry.

This is a prerequisite exercise before you begin your meditations.

Seeing the *White Light*

Let's go back to the *White Light* and begin by sitting or lying down, so that your spine is straight. You will close your eyes and slowly breathe in through your nose, counting to six. As you breathe in, behind your closed eyes, visualize a bright column of *White Light* above your head.

Meditation - The Master Key

If you cannot see it as a column and it appears as a white cloud or spot light, that is fine. No matter what form it is in, that is perfect for you at this time. Then begin to slowly exhale through your mouth again counting to six. As you exhale, visualize the *White Light* coming down through the top of your head through your frontal lobe or crown chakra.

You then take another deep breath, breathing in slowly and watching the *White Light* going down through your body. You will exhale again and move the light down to your legs.

On your third breath visualize the *White Light* moving down your legs and out your feet. As you exhale watch the light encircle your body and create a bubble around you. Then breathe normally and see yourself sitting or lying inside a big white bubble.

Now let's go through the meditation process. . .

White Bubble

The following meditation script is intended to guide you through the process. You may want to have a partner read it to you or you can purchase our **Peaceful White Light tapes** with the order blank at the back of the book. Choose a quiet place, turn off your radio and TV.

Allow yourself to relax in a chair or lie down. Arms down to your sides, palms facing upward. Move your feet apart, so that the thighs are not touching.

Focus on your feet, let them go limp.

Become aware of your calves, tell the muscles to relax.

Let your knees relax. Relax your thighs.

Feel your legs getting very heavy and melting down, down, into the floor.

In your mind, picture your spine. See it very straight and put a long golden cord alongside your spine, holding it in place. Now, you can allow the muscles in your back to relax and melt down, down into the floor.

Move around to your abdomen and let it go, feeling as though you have a great deal of room for all of your organs to do their work. See all your vital organs pulsating and doing their job with energy and plenty of room. There is no constriction.

Move up to your chest area and let it go. Take a deep breath and release the tension in your chest area. Move to your heart and feel it beating. Listen to your heartbeat. Feel it slowing to a nice rhythmic beat where you are feeling very comfortable and relaxed.

Meditation - The Master Key

Move up to your shoulders and let them drop down. As they are dropping down, your arms and hands are getting very heavy. Your whole body is melting down into the floor and you are going deeper and deeper into relaxation.

Roll your neck from side to side feeling all the stress and tension rolling out of your neck, leaving it feeling so relaxed and free. Let your neck fall wherever it feels comfortable.

Drop your jaw down and swing it from side to side. Gently and easily take a deep yawn. As you do this you will go into a deep relaxation.

Spread your nostrils and take in a deep breath. Breathe in through your nose with the nostrils spread wide and exhale through your mouth.

Feel the palms of my hands across your eyes. The warmth of my palms will soothe away any tension or stress in your eyes leaving your eyes feeling relaxed and allowing the stress to melt away.

Feel my fingertips going across your forehead, wiping away all of your problems. Let your problems and worries fall onto the floor next to you.

Your mind is feeling so relaxed and clear. Your body is completely relaxed.

I want you to take in three deep breaths. Breathe in through your nose only, and exhale from your mouth. As you are breathing in, visualize a beam of **White Light** *coming down through the top of your head. It can be like a bright spotlight, or a white puffy cloud, however you imagine it.*

Let's begin: Breathe in deeply through your nose and see or feel your magnificent **White Light** *. Exhale through your mouth slowly.*

Take another deep breath through your nose and feel the beautiful **White Light** *move down your body. Exhale slowly through your mouth.*

Breathe in again and bring the **White Light** *down through the body and out your feet, encircling your entire body and exhale. You are now completely encircled in* **White Light** *.*

This is your own private **White Light** *bubble. It is pure positive energy. This positive energy will fill your electrical system, making you feel safe, secure and happy.*

Now that you are in this lovely **White Light** *bubble, allow yourself to feel free, let yourself go ,and travel to wherever you want. Maybe you would like to visit a relative or fly over the countryside; or just be in your private* **White Light** *bubble and enjoy the peacefulness.*

This is a safe place for you to be. If you begin to experience things such as a picture or a feeling, remember everything that you encounter.

Do not look for anything. Just let it come to you. Allow the pictures or feelings or perhaps smells come to you, do not look for them. Do not try to see or feel, but instead allow it to flow to you. Relax.

(You can meditate 5 to 15 minutes)

Close your hands and make a fist.

Meditation - The Master Key

*Breathe in through your nose and visualize the **White Light** coming down in a column through the top of your head. Exhale through your mouth.*

Breathe in again through your nose, exhale through your mouth. One last time, breath in deeply and hold it, hold it, and exhale quickly through your mouth.

You are feeling calm, refreshed, and relaxed. Open your eyes slowly and very slowly sit up. Do not talk to anyone. Write down what you experienced in the meditation Journal at the end of this chapter.

Making a Tape

If you do not have my **Peaceful White Light meditation tapes** you can make your own by recording the above meditation script. If you find that silence does not work for you, then put on some music that makes you feel relaxed.

Write in your meditation journal section what you experienced. Even if you just saw a color, put that down. Remember to date and put the time down in your meditation journal. It may seem unimportant at the time, but later you might have a verification on your meditation.

Meditation Journal

Meditation   **Day**_____   **Time** _____

_____

_____

_____

_____

_____

_____

_____

_____

_____

_____

_____

_____

_____

_____

_____

Chapter 5

Telepathy or Sending Thoughts

Telepathy : apparent communication from one mind to another other than through the channels of the senses

Maybe you have experienced mental telepathy. It could have been when you wanted your spouse to bring home a loaf of bread and a quart of milk. It could have been a telephone call to your mother. Reflect on some past "telepathic" experience you have had.

Experience:

_____

_____

_____

_____

_____

_____

ESP - Finally, the Proof

The existence of psychic powers such as telepathy has been a hard thing for mainstream scientists to accept, partly because so - called "objective" proofs in the past have often taken the form of poorly defined studies coupled with a big dose of wishful thinking. Many cases of cheating and outright fraud have further undermined credibility. Now, however, experimental work on psi effects by researchers from Cornell University and the University of Edinburgh in Scotland, is finally bringing some respect to the field. A study describing the work was published in the American Psychological Association's Psychological Bulletin, having passed a peer-review process prior to publication.

Proof in psi research is usually a matter of beating the odds. If researchers can observe that a phenomenon happens more frequently than it would by chance, then it is assumed that there is some influence such as psychic phenomenon at work. And, this is what took place in the ground-breaking psi study.

Researchers had two people sit in acoustically sealed rooms. The "sender" would concentrate on one of 80 still pictures, or one of 80 short video clips, and the "receiver" would attempt to pick out the target image on a computer screen among three decoys. By the laws of chance, the receiver should only be able to pick out the correct image one-in-four times. Yet, in a statistical analysis of over 11 studies, receivers scored a "hit" about every third session, a statistically significant effect.

In one study using art students, the hit rate was one-in-two, the highest ever recorded in this type of study. Creative abilities and an extroverted personality type are thought to boost psi performance.

Telepathy

This particular psi experiment employed what is called the ganzfeld ("whole") procedure. Receivers wear eye coverings and white-noise earphones, and relaxation exercises are performed prior to reception. By shutting out external sensory stimulation, and reducing muscular tensions, receivers are thought to be more able to detect normally weak psi information. More studies are underway to try to replicate these provocative research findings.

We are now ready to begin our first experience into **"Your Psychic World."** Remember there are three important processes to practice.

- **Meditation**
- *White Light*
- **Visualizations**

Throughout the years of teaching, I have found that if these three processes don't occur in the beginning of each session, my students have great difficulty attaining their goals. They became disturbed, disjointed, and melancholy. I cannot emphasis enough how important these three steps are.

If you follow these processes before beginning the exercises, you will have excellent results. Not only will you benefit in developing your psychic awareness, but you will also learn to relax without having to spend a few hours sleeping.

I have had many students bothered by nervous disorders, such as recover from a nervous breakdown, shingles, rashes, allergies, stress, high blood pressure, diabetes, hives, ticks, irritability, depression, even severe constipation and solving problems. After practicing the relaxing meditation process, their conditions disappeared.

Several doctors called me and asked what I was doing to help create this type of healing in their patient. Some other comments students have made were, **"I have been able to solve problems so much easier." "I don't need to take naps like I used to, when I'm tired." "When I meditate, it makes me feel alive and full of energy." "I feel so relaxed and able to cope with my family problems. The children don't upset me like they used to." "I can make better judgments at work. New ideas just seem to come so easily."**

One of the constant complaints of people is, "I don't have time to sit and meditate. I am just too busy." Well, my answer to that is, you don't have to spend hours meditating, it only takes a few minutes.

One of my suggestions to a very busy executive was, "Go into the bathroom and sit for five minutes, if this is all the time you have." Several weeks later, he confessed, "Annette, that really works. And I feel terrific and not as stressed out, like I used to be."

What Is Telepathy?

Telepathy is sending mental messages or thoughts of any kind from one person to another without the apparent use of the physical senses. This has also been called thought transference. I prefer to call it sending.

Telepathy (far-feeling) is the direct communication, voluntarily or involuntary, of one mind with another. It is the thoughts of one person (the sender) who is sending or beaming to the conscious mind of another (the receiver), rather like a radio or television signal traveling from the transmitting station to the appropriate aerial.

Telepathy

Telepathic communication can bridge vast distances without losing it's force, it is instantaneous and is unimpeded by any known physical wall or barrier. Some believe that telepathy is the synchronous growth of the same idea or set of ideas in two minds at the same time. One of these minds may well be the agent or sender, the other the receiver or percipient, but to all intents and purposes each mind generates the same thought or thoughts independently of the other. Nothing, travels between them.

Telepathy is not a mental capacity that has been recently discovered or wondered about, even though it is only during the last hundred years that it has been experimentally investigated. Mankind's recognition of it is extremely ancient, it's occurrence was usually attributed to a god or spirit, who was believed to have passed on the thoughts of person A to person B. Indeed, our telepathic, clairvoyant and precognitive abilities appear to have atrophied in modern time, when we have become cut off from the rhythms of nature, from quietness and inner peace, and from an acceptance of the possibilities of such things, all of which heighten extra-sensory perception.

Families of primitive tribes often possess quite remarkable powers in this respect, to the extent of knowing what a distant tribesman is doing, the whereabouts of game, water and other non-observable necessities, and the outcome of a particular course of action; talents that are generally reduced or lost completely when they become "civilized."

Telepathic communication, perhaps hardly surprisingly, is strongest between mother and child, and there are numerous accounts of a mother sensing when something is happening to her offspring.

Here Is an Example of Telepathy Between Mother and Son

One morning a young mother was driving her six-year-old son to school. It was raining and they got caught in a traffic jam. Waiting and getting more frustrated at getting her son to school late, she thought to herself, "Wouldn't it be wonderful to just be able to fly over the traffic and get Scott to school on time." Scott turned to his mother and replied, "Mommy, if we fly, you will scare all of the people in the other cars and maybe have an accident."

We are going to experience what we have just been talking about by going through experiential exercises. After awhile, with practice you will be able to turn your sixth sense on and off like a light switch.

Exercise 1
Sending a color
This requires a partner (two adults, two children, adult and child)

Selecting the person to work with you is very important. Try to find someone who is genuinely interested in and not antagonistic to the psychic world. If the person you select is not in harmony with you or the exercise, this could create problems in accuracy. Make sure you take the phone off the hook, the radio is off, and you will not be disturbed during the exercise.

✔❏ Sit on the floor or in chairs facing each other. Decide which person is going to be the Sender of the color and which person will be the Receiver. Enter your names in the following score sheet. Hold hands.

Telepathy

✔️❑ Do the following Sender / Receiver exercise four times.

✔️❑ **Sender:** Think of a color. See it in your mind. Feel the color if you can. Put it into a ball and see the colored ball in your hands. If you are a person who does not see, repeat the color over in your mind. Just keep focusing on the color of the ball. *Do not think any other thoughts!*

✔️❑ **Receiver** Close your eyes and take in your three deep breaths. Breathing through your nose and bringing in the *White Light* as you breathe. Allow the *White Light* to create a bubble around you. Exhale through your mouth.

In your mind see a blank movie screen. Allow the color to come over to you onto your screen. Once you feel that you are experiencing the color, either by seeing, feeling, tasting, smelling, or just knowing what color it is, tell your partner what you are experiencing. The most important part of this exercise is to tell your partner everything you are experiencing.

Your greatest accuracy will be on the first thing you see, feel, hear, taste, smell, or know. Do not be afraid to tell your partner what you are experiencing.

✔️❑ **Sender** Give your partner verbal feedback. Keep focusing on the color until your partner gets it.

✔️❑ **Receiver** If you have not come up with the correct color within three tries, quit! If you get the correct color then switch and let the other person be the receiver.

✔️❑ Congratulate your partner for a job well done! Positive and enthusiastic feedback is very important in your development.

The two partners should go through the same process of breathing and taking in the *White Light* . It is most important since this clears your mind, protects you, and helps to focus your subconscious on the exercise. Bring up the movie screen, let that take the place, momentarily, of your busy conscious mind. **Practice makes perfect!**

Record your color sending accuracy

Date _____

Sender's Name _____ Receiver's Name _____

Color sent 1. _____ 2. _____ 3. _____

Color received 1. _____ 2. _____ 3. _____

Sender's Name _____ Receiver's Name _____

Color sent 1. _____ 2. _____ 3. _____

Color received 1. _____ 2. _____ 3. _____

Telepathy

Exercise 2
Sending colors with colored paper
This requires a partner (two adults, two children, adult and child)

✔❏ You will need five sheets of different colored paper, such as red, blue, green, yellow, pink, orange, brown, black.

✔❏ Sit on the floor or in chairs, with your backs to each other. Decide which person will be the Sender of the color and which person will be the Receiver. Enter your names in the following score sheet.

✔❏ Do the following Sender / Receiver exercise two times.

✔❏ **Sender** Put all the colors in front of you. Close your eyes and choose one swatch. Put the rest of the colors back in the pouch or cover them, so that you cannot see them. Hold the color you have chosen in front of your eyes and focus only on that color.

✔❏ **Receiver** Take your three deep breaths, bring in the *White Light.* Breathe in through your nose and exhale through your mouth. Relax and allow the movie screen to come up. Now allow the color to come on to your screen. You may not see it, but you could feel, know, smell, taste the color. It could remind you of a food, a flower, sky, or even a sound. Whatever the very first impression is, tell your partner. *Remember, it is usually your first impression that is correct.*

✔❏ **Sender** Give your partner feedback. Yes, that is true. Or no, try again. If after three tries, your partner cannot see the color, quit! If you make a hit, it means you got it right. Mark it on your score on the next page.

✔❏ Switch Sender and Receiver and repeat the above. Do three colors.

Record your color sending accuracy

Date _____

Sender's Name _____ Receiver's Name _____

Color sent   1. _____   2. _____   3. _____

Color received   1. _____   2. _____   3. _____

Sender's Name _____ Receiver's Name _____

Color sent   1. _____   2. _____   3. _____

Color received   1. _____   2. _____   3. _____

Telepathy

Homework

1. Meditate each day for at least five minutes using the technique we have learned in this section. Remember to always use the *White Light*, when meditating and beginning each exercise.

2. Do the exercise of sending the colors and writing your scores in the book. This is to show you how you are progressing. It is important for you to have positive feedback.

Choose a partner to work with. Set a time and day of the next week, where you will send three colors to your partner. Write down in your book, if you are to be the Sender or the Receiver and record your color.

Date _____

Sender's Name _____ Receiver's Name _____

Color sent 1. _____ 2. _____ 3. _____

Color received 1. _____ 2. _____ 3. _____

Sender's Name _____ Receiver's Name _____

Color sent 1. _____ 2. _____ 3. _____

Color received 1. _____ 2. _____ 3. _____

If you are working alone, put each color swatch into an envelope. Close your eyes and choose an envelope. Keep your eyes closed, take your three deep breaths, and bring in the *White Light*. Relax and bring up your white movie screen. Allow the color to come to you. Write it in this book on line one. Open your envelope and see how well you did. Do two more the same way. You can practice this as often as you like.

There have been studies done with the blind where they have learned to see the colors with their hands. Amazing, isn't it? You can learn to do this as well. Practice.

3. If for some reason you are having trouble, go back to where you were doing well and work on that particular area. Then go on to something new.

You have completed the first section in

"Discovering Your Psychic World."

Chapter 6

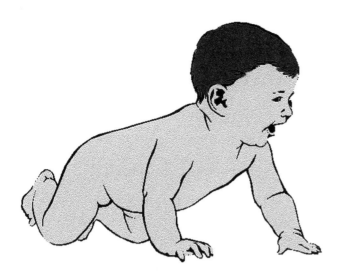

Steps into Your Psychic World

The baby first learns to crawl, then stands, and finally takes the first step.

Building self esteem and confidence will help us to self-awareness. We need to remember to :

- *Prepare your body*
  - **Relax** and **let go** of the physical body.
  - **Be sensitive** to your body sensations, like a warm or cold feeling.
  - **Breathe** deeply.
  - **Allow** yourself to feel.
  - **Listen** with your gut feelings.
  - **Listen** to messages giving you positive feedback or warning you to be careful.
  - **Watch** your mental pictures, they are elusive and fleeting at times.

- *Prepare your mind*
  - **Let go** of your expectations.
  - **Have patience** with yourself.
  - **Stop** the chattering conscious mind.
  - **Bring in** the energy of the White Light .
  - **Allow** the light to be within and light the way for you.
  - **Trust** what is happening to you-no matter what.
  - **Be aware** of difference between your imagination and intuition.
  - **Feel safe** at all times.
  - **Do not** criticize yourself.
  - **Give** yourself positive feedback.
  - **Love** and like yourself.
  - **Do not hold** onto old methods of doing things.
  - **Let your ego go** and not be afraid that it is gone forever.

Steps into Your Psychic World

- *Increase your intuition*
  - **Let** the information come to you softly.
  - **Not try** to force yourself into seeing.
  - Always **practice with positive** thoughts, never bring harm or pain on someone else.
  - **Open** yourself and give, without asking for anything in return.
  - **Focus** the unconscious, subconscious mind.
  - **Pay attention** when someone is talking to you.
  - Know that **nothing is impossible,** only our limited perception holds us back.

- *Handle intuitive information*
  - **Understand** the difference between your stuff and theirs.
  - **It is not** a new toy.
  - Only **with permission** enter another being's consciousness.
  - **Realize** is not against God or church.
  - **Not show off** with accomplishments.
  - **Laugh** at yourself - don't take yourself too seriously.
  - **Understand** that there is no time and you can move from past, present, and future.
  - **Be responsible** for self alone.
  - **Let go** of information. Once it is given let it dissipate. Do not hold onto it. You are merely reflecting back to the person, like a mirror, what is already there.
  - Always **leave** them with White Light, pure positive energy.
  - **Give** the information in a caring, loving way.
  - **Not filter or change** the information out of fear that it will upset the person.
  - **Learn** to speak their language.

Helping to Regulate Your Energy

Before we begin our meditation we are going to do another breathing technique. This particular type of breathing will help you to have more **energy**.

Take your left hand and put your left thumb to block the left nostril. The rest of the fingers on your left hand should be straight up. Now simply inhale and exhale through the right nostril only, for one to three minutes.

After three minutes, you will feel totally revitalized. This is a yogic breathing technique and it can work as a coffee substitute.

If you don't have time to meditate and **need to calm yourself** because you might be going to the dentist, speaking in front of a group, or just nervous about a situation, try this:

Block the right nostril with the right thumb. Inhale and exhale through the left nostril only, for one to three minutes.

Steps into Your Psychic World

Remember to Use Your Breath

Let's talk a little more about our deep breathing, as we did in Chapter 1. Practice long, deep breathing often. You can even practice while driving in the car or walking, standing in line at the grocery store, or playing with your toddler. Check yourself throughout the day. Is your breathing shallow? Breathe deeply!

The Benefits of Deep Breathing

The more you practice this long, deep breathing regularly, your lung capacity will increase, the pituitary gland will secrete many hormones that govern vital processes in the body, and the intuitional or survival senses will begin to develop. Long, deep breathing helps to stimulate the production of chemicals in the brain, called endorphins, that eliminate the tendency to depression. This is the same high euphoric feeling athletes get after running.

Another plus of deep breathing is that it helps to regulate the body's pH (acid/alkalinity), which affects our ability to handle stressful situations. Also, by filling your lungs to capacity, you will be strengthening your electromagnetic field. This will be of great assistance in lowering your susceptibility to accidents, sickness, and negativity.

If you continue to practice this deep breathing it will create a definite effect on your subconscious. The breathing will also be beneficial in breaking undesirable habits and addictions.

So Remember to Breathe Deep!

Magical Garden Journey

Please follow the Meditation Process in Chapter 4 as a prelude to the following visualization process. Again, you may have a partner read the following script, you may tape it ahead of time, or you may purchase all of the meditations and visualizations from Artistic Visions with the order blank in the back of this book. The larger bolded words should be read more loudly.

Gently concentrate on seeing a blank white movie screen in front of your eyes.

The two most important things in developing yourself are: Believing & Trusting in what you see, hear, feel, taste, and smell! It takes time but slowly things will start to come to you.

You will remember everything that you experience.

We are going to take a journey into a magical garden.

In the distance is a gate and as you walk up to it, your eyes are filled with the color radiating out from this beautiful garden full of flowers. Look at all those beautiful flowers! Let's walk over to one of them. Put one in your hand and with the other hand touch the petals. Run your fingers over the petals and see how they feel. Are they soft? Maybe they are very prickly. Look closely at the petals.

Remember what it looks like.

Steps into Your Psychic World

Bring the flower to your nose and smell it. What does it smell like?

Remember the smell.

Now look closer inside the petals and see if there are any seeds in there. Feel the seeds with your fingers. What color are they?

Remember what colors you saw.

It's time now to make yourself very small so that we can travel down the stem of this beautiful flower. Go down the outside the stem and walk on one of the leaves. Put your hands down and feel the edge of the leaf. What is it like? Is it straight and smooth or is it rough and jagged? Feel it.

Remember what it feels like.

Travel down the rest of the stem. You can go either down the outside or the inside of the stem.

Go down, down to the earth. I want you to walk around the earth. What color is it? What does it look like? Now get on all fours and put your nose down to the earth and smell it. What does it smell like? Is it dry? Or maybe it's been freshly watered.

Remember the smell of the earth.

Imagine yourself burrowing through the earth beneath your beautiful flowers. Now crawl around the roots of this plant. My goodness, what color are the roots? Is the ground a different color than before? What does it smell like down there?

Do you see any critters wandering around down there? If you do, go up to them and observe them. They won't hurt you. They are as curious about you as you are of them.

Remember what they look like.

Say good-bye to your new-found friends for it is time for us to climb back up the roots to the stem of your flower. You can travel back up the stem either on the outside or the inside. Go up, up, above the ground.

Feel yourself growing bigger and bigger back to your normal body size. You are standing looking at your magical flower garden. Allow any thoughts or pictures to come across your screen. Let them gently come in and go out, stay very relaxed.

Watch the pictures and remember them.

You are feeling wonderful and peaceful. Turn and walk out of your magical garden for now. Remember this beautiful place, for you can always return anytime you want.

Feel yourself coming back into the room again and into your body. Feel your body lying on the floor.. Close your hands and make a fist. This will circulate the energy within your own body and help to regenerate you.

Visualize your White Light and take in your three deep breaths. Breathe in through your nose and exhale through your mouth.

Steps into Your Psychic World

Breathe in.   Bring the White Light in through the top of your head.   Exhale.

Breathe in.   Bring the White Light down your body.   Exhale

Breathe in one more time and feel the White Light circulating around your body.   And quickly exhale. Return to regular breathing.

Gently open your eyes and very slowly sit up. Do not talk. Write down everything that you experienced. If you feel dizzy after any meditation or visualization, close your eyes and take another few deep breaths while telling yourself to come back straight into your body.

Use the following Meditation Journal and write down everything that you experienced.

Meditation Journal

Meditation   Date _____   Time _____

_____
_____
_____
_____
_____
_____
_____
_____
_____
_____
_____
_____
_____
_____
_____
_____
_____
_____
_____
_____
_____
_____
_____
_____
_____
_____
_____
_____
_____
_____
_____

Benefits

Here are some major benefits of developing our sixth sense

<u>Health</u>

- ꝕ Illness is subdued.
- ꝕ You can understand and control your pain much easier.
- ꝕ You will sleep better.
- ꝕ Even your complexion will begin to change for the better.
- ꝕ Your health will improve as you become more aware of self.
- ꝕ Your circulation will improve.
- ꝕ Your stress will begin to disappear.

<u>Mind</u>

- ꝕ You will have a new outlook on life.
- ꝕ Your perception of the world will be different.
- ꝕ You will be solving problems in another way.
- ꝕ Your perception of self will be more open and flexible.
- ꝕ You will begin to make decisions in a different gut-level approach.
- ꝕ You can understand complicated aspects better.
- ꝕ The understanding of: Yes, we do come in the world alone and leave alone, but we now have more opportunities to have a better understanding of all of our relationships.
- ꝕ You will explore the inner regions of your fantastic mind.

<u>Emotions</u>

- ꝕ Your listening capabilities will be more acute.
- ꝕ There will be a better understanding of your feelings.
- ꝕ You will have a new sense of freedom.
- ꝕ Your optimism will be stronger than before.
- ꝕ You will be more outgoing and not afraid to express yourself.
- ꝕ You will have a clearer picture of where you want to go with your life.
- ꝕ You will learn not to take responsibility for anyone else but yourself.
- ꝕ Your communication with loved ones and co-workers will improve.
- ꝕ You will begin to smile more.
- ꝕ Your inner child will surface.

Chapter 7

Sending Emotions & Pictures

Our next step in developing our ability to "see" beyond our eyes will be to explore sensing emotions and pictures transmitted from another person. You have probably "seen" emotions being sent from another person without realizing it. A quick glance at a person's facial expression probably confirmed what you had already known.

First we are going to practice sending and receiving emotions Then we will progress to more advanced steps of transmitting and receiving pictures. You will be surprised that all of this is possible with just a little practice and a positive, can-do attitude. As you practice these exercises it will be like turning on and off a light switch.

Exercise 1
Sending emotions
This requires a partner (two adults, two children, adult and child)

Make sure you take the phone off the hook, the radio is off, and you will not be disturbed during the exercise.

✔❑ Sit on the floor or in chairs, with your backs to each other. Decide which person will be the Sender and who will be the Receiver. Enter your names in the following score sheet.

✔❑ No talking during this exercise.

✔❑ Put a time clock out for yourselves and **set it for 10 minutes.**

✔❑ Do the following Sender / Receiver exercise once.

Sending Emotions & Pictures

✔❏ **Sender** Choose an emotion. It can be any human emotion such as happiness, anger, disgust, jealousy, envy, sympathy, etc.

Record your emotion on the Sender section of the score sheet. Make it simple! Choose only one emotion. Concentrate only on the emotion you have selected, nothing else.

✔❏ **Receiver** Close your eyes and begin your breathing. Breathe in through your nose and bring in the *White Light* . Exhale through your mouth. Do this exercise three times.

Bring up your blank, white movie screen. Take a few more breaths if you need too and allow the emotion to come over to you. Allow the emotion to come to you. Be gentle with yourself, be kind to yourself. If you try to make it happen, it will not work.

When we try or force ourselves to do anything we are then creating a resistance. This is applicable to everything in life. So pay attention to what it is you are doing. When you begin to get an impression, write down the name of the emotion on a blank piece of paper.

✔❏ Mark your score down on the following page and discuss what you experienced with your partner for a few moments.

✔❏ Switch Sender and Receiver.

✔❏ Repeat the process . Put down your score and discuss your progress.

Record your emotion-sending accuracy

Date _____

Sender's Name _____ Receiver's Name _____

Emotion sent 1. _____ 2. _____ 3. _____

Emotion received 1. _____ 2. _____ 3. _____

Sender's Name _____ Receiver's Name _____

Emotion sent 1. _____ 2. _____ 3. _____

Emotion received 1. _____ 2. _____ 3. _____

Sending Emotions & Pictures

Example of sending a drawn picture

All pictures in this segment were drawn and sent by my students.

Sender

Receiver

Sending Emotions & Pictures

<table>
<tr><td>

Exercise 4
Sending a drawing
This requires a partner (two adults, two children, adult and child)

</td></tr>
</table>

✔❑ You will need blank white paper and drawing utensils.

✔❑ Sit on the floor or in chairs, with your backs to each other. Decide who will be the Sender of the symbol and who will be the Receiver. Enter your names in the following score sheet.

✔❑ There is to be no talking during this exercise.

✔❑ Each obtain a blank 8 1/2 by 11-inch or larger piece of paper. Use a hard surface to draw on, like a clipboard. You can also use a sketch pad that has a heavier paper. Use a pencil or pen that is dark enough to show on the paper. If you are artistic, you could even paint in water colors or pen and ink, whatever you feel comfortable using.

✔❑ Put a time clock out for yourselves and **set it for 10 minutes.**

✔❑ Do the following Sender / Receiver exercise.

✔❑ Show your partner what you drew. Discuss both your impressions.

✔❑ Switch Sender and Receiver.

✔❑ Put what was sent and what was received in your notebook.

✔❑ You can do this exercise twice. Then you will begin to get tired. Do not overdue in hopes that practicing repeatedly that day will develop the skill, immediately, it will not! You will just over-tax your mind. It will be fun and instant feedback for you to be able to see your impressions on the paper. The more positive the feedback the quicker you will learn and want to go on to better things.

✔❑ **Sender** Think of a situation that you have been in that is highly charged with emotion. Remember it in your mind. Take time to think about it and then draw it on your piece of paper. Make it large enough, use the whole page.

Draw the scene where this emotion occurred. This could be a place that you enjoy relaxing in, like the mountains, going fishing, skiing, swimming, hiking, whatever. The most important thing is to choose a scene that means something to you. Once you finish the picture, keep drawing over it. Concentrate on the picture, see yourself there, feel yourself there and the emotions you felt while in this special place.

Keep reliving it again and concentrate.

Sending Emotions & Pictures

✔❑ **Receiver** Close your eyes and take in your three deep breaths. Breathe in through your nose, bringing the *White Light* down through the top of your head and exhale through your mouth. Do this three times.

Bring up your blank, white movie screen. Take a few more breaths if you need too and allow the picture to come over to you on your screen. You may have some emotions about the scene you are experiencing. If you have trouble drawing them, write the words down on the paper.

Remember the first impressions are usually the right impressions.

Even if it seems silly to you, put it down on the paper. If you are having difficulty picking up anything, take another couple of deep breaths, always using the *White Light*. The *White Light* will help to clear your conscious mind of cluttered thoughts.

Close your hands, making a fist. Bring in the *White Light* again, taking your three deep breaths and exhale quickly on the third breath. This will clear your mind and help you to let go of the scene.

Record your accuracy in sending a drawing

Date _____

Sender's Name _____ Receiver's Name _____

Picture sent   1. _____ 2. _____ 3. _____

Picture received   1. _____ 2. _____ 3. _____

Sender's Name _____ Receiver's Name _____

Picture sent   1. _____ 2. _____ 3. _____

Picture received   1. _____ 2. _____ 3. _____

Sending Emotions & Pictures

Here are more examples of sending and receiving drawn pictures. Examine them carefully and observe how the exact picture was being transferred from mind to mind.

Sender

Receiver

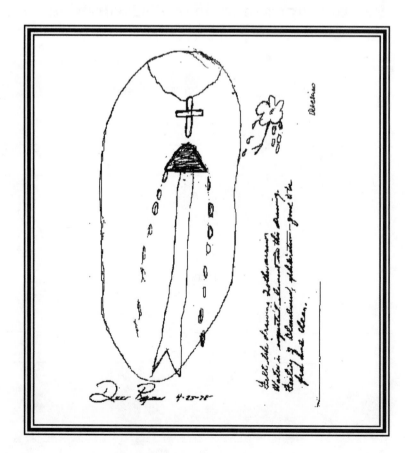

Sending Emotions & Pictures

Sender

Receiver

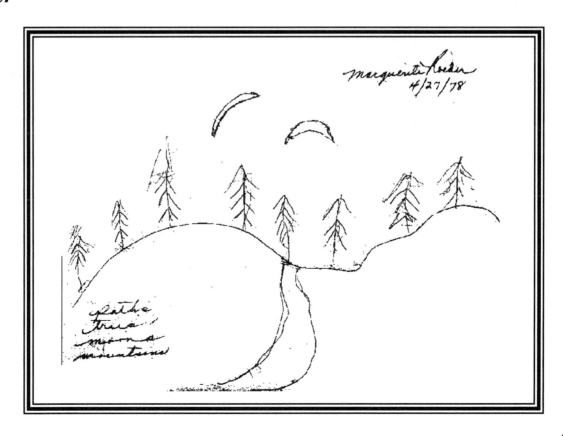

Sending Emotions & Pictures

Sender

Receiver

Sending Emotions & Pictures

Sender

Receiver

Sending Emotions & Pictures

Sender

Receiver

As you can see, this type of sending can be done. Our minds are incredible and these types of exercises prove it!

Sending Emotions & Pictures

Homework

1. Choose a partner to work with. Set a time and day in the next week where you will send an emotion to your partner.

2. Write down in your book if you are to be the Sender or the Receiver.

3. Call your partner at the designated time and send the selected emotion if you are the Sender.

4. If you are the Receiver, keep your eyes closed, take your three deep breaths, and bring in the *White Light*. Relax and bring up your screen. Allow the emotion to come to you. Write it in this book. Do two more the same way. You can practice this as often as you like.

Date _____

Sender's Name _____   Receiver's Name _____

Emotion sent _____   Emotion received _____

Emotion sent _____   Emotion received _____

Emotion sent _____   Emotion received _____

Date _____

Sender's Name _____   Receiver's Name _____

Emotion sent _____   Emotion received _____

Emotion sent _____   Emotion received _____

Emotion sent _____   Emotion received _____

Chapter 8

What Is This Thing Called the Aura?

People have talked about the aura in terms of, "My goodness, that person has an air about him (or her)." Or we will say that a person gives off a strange vibration or definitely has "bad vibes." These are perceptions people make about others every day and yet intuitively we use this information to guide our actions and decisions.

Frequently, we act on these gut-level perceptions to decide whether we will trust someone, or perhaps what the person is saying. We also make decisions about the kind of energy we want to be around at that particular moment.

In 500 BC. Pythagoras wrote about a light radiating from humans that was said to be responsible for a variety of physical effects. The scholars in the twelfth century agreed that one person can affect another simply by the presence of the energy emanating from his body.

Where Does the Word Aura Come from?
The word aura comes from the Greek meaning "breath" or "air." The dictionary defines aura as:
  1) Any subtle, invisible emanation or exhalation such as the aura or scent of flowers.
  2) A distinctive atmosphere surrounding a person; such as an aura of sanctity.
  3) A draft or motion of air caused by electrical repulsion.

Simply put, an aura is the electromagnetic or energy field that surrounds every living thing. It is an invisible body print that surrounds us at all times. It is changing constantly according to what we are thinking, feeling, and our state of health, and it responds to energies around us.

Psychic Exploration by astronaut Edgar D. Mitchell, explains: "The aura is an envelope or field of colored energy or radiation said by sensitives to surround the human body. It has colors indicative of different aspects of the person's physical, psychological, and spiritual condition. Some traditions hold that there is more than one aura within the total envelope, each having distinctive properties."

What Is The Aura?

Can We Measure the Aura?

The aura, or electromagnetic field, is a measurable emanation. It gives off both light and heat. The heat can be measured through a heat- sensing process and the light through a photographic process. If we could film or video tape our aura, we would see that it is constantly in motion. It is organic in that it is part of us. The aura changes as we pass through our different moods and feelings.

When we are happy it will be large and bright. But, when we are sad or ill, the aura will grow small and dark. When we are angry or fearful, the aura will be shrunken inward. If we continue to stay in a negative state for a long period of time, an imbalance manifests with the physical body. This is a definite sign to the individual that something has gone wrong in his or her thinking and usually requires an attitudinal change to readjust the energy and reconstruct a healthy aura.

What Size Is the Aura?

The aura is never consistent in size and shape. It could bulge and bubble in different places. Sometimes it will be a round shape or conical shape over the top of the head. Or there could be a large bulge over the right ear or left side of the body. These energies are constantly shifting, creating different shapes as it moves around.

The size of the aura or electromagnetic field will depend upon the species of the living organism. Bugs have a smaller field, as they are small and simple beings. As living things become more complex biologically, they will tend to have more energy. The more energy a human has, the larger and more visible the auric field. Our plants are likely to have smaller auras than our pets. The pets are likely to have smaller auras than the humans.

Kirlin Photography

For those who are skeptical, this emanation can be seen by a special process called Kirlin photography, named for the Russian scientist who discovered it. Kirlin discovered that by running high frequency electrical fields through living things and varying the frequencies, different details show up in the photographs. An electromagnetic halo projecting from the human body and other life forms will show on infrared film. Kirlin research suggests that the aura can be brighter and larger when a person is in meditation or prayer. An early warning system for disease can be shown by a disturbance in the energy patterns.

Newer Discoveries

Energy Research Group of New York City has developed a method of viewing the human aura on video tape. This group of scientists reports that "a thin pulsating field was displayed around the human body." We all have a white field of energy that lies close to our bodies. The aura field just beyond this white begins to change shape and pulsate constantly. Here is where we begin to see colors. The colors are not solid but rather of light. You may not always see the colors, but *sense* them instead.

How does light travel? Light travels in waves. When the *White Light* is broken down into its components, as through a prism, we can then see the colors of the spectrum. A beautiful rainbow is merely the separation of light into individual frequencies. It is important to remember that each color has its own frequency and together these frequencies constitute the magnificent and brilliant *White Light* .

What Is The Aura?

The colors we sense, or see, are in constant movement according to our physical, emotional, and mental health. When our lives are terrific, the aura appears to be bright and large with clear colors emanating. If we are out of sorts, the aura will become less solid and the colors will be murky and dull. A happy person will emanate an almost opaque aura, reflecting solid energy. If you are ill or unhappy, the aura will be thin and sometimes rough and jagged looking.

As you become aware of your aura, you can change the shape and the size of it at will. All you need to do is concentrate with focused intent and visualize a change in your aura.

When I find myself in a negative situation, I begin to focus on the *White Light* and consciously expand my aura. This creates a protected space for me, so that I am not bombarded by negativity. When we speak, we are sending our auras outward toward the listener. Sometimes we can see this mental energy coming out of the forehead just above the nose, which is called the "third eye." Following is my chart of the colors and the roles they play in our aura or electromagnetic field.

Annette Martin's Color Chart

I have been using this color chart for the past 23 years. It has proven to be quite accurate. These colors can be seen either in the aura or inside the body. The darker the color, the more intense the meaning. The lighter the color, the less intense.

BLUE — Beginning Awareness

Beginning to awaken to ourselves and the world around us. This color has more to do with our spiritual side than physical.

GREEN — Healing

When seen in certain areas of the body, this area is being worked on by the subconscious mind. The person is working on a subconscious level to heal themselves. You can heal yourself through your thoughts. Green is in the middle of the color spectrum and it represents balance. Green is the color of nature. It provides peace, harmony and healing to the nervous system.

YELLOW — Self-Awareness

We might say a person with a sunshine personality. Optimism prevails. It is also the color of the intellect, so people who are mentally active tend to show a great deal of yellow in their auras.

LAVENDER or PURPLE — Changes

There are changes going on and depending where the color is seen you can see what is changing. For example, the liver is purple, this means that the person is changing habits of eating and drinking. Purple is a strong healing color. It is the highest vibration of light and is frequently associated with mysticism. Purple is a wonderful color for mental equilibrium and has to do with spiritual development and clairvoyance.

RED — Anger

You will usually see this color in dots and sometimes streaks. For example, If a person has a bad foot and all you see is red around the foot, you will know that the person has transferred other anger to that area and caused it to flare up. The color red also denotes INSANITY! This is only true when seen around the head area. It can jut out in streaks, splotches, or big circles. You will know that this person is unfit to make decisions or judgments about self.

What Is The Aura?

When there is a dark red, we instantly know that there is a great deal of anger. You have heard the expression, "He was so angry he saw red." What this means is that this anger made the aura very strong and, therefore, visible. A clear, bright red is energy at its highest physical point. This red energy can move boulders or large objects, participate in athletics, or perform lengthy physical feats.

We have all read stories where the mother comes out front to find her child pinned under a car. She runs over to the car, raises up the vehicle with her bare hands, and pulls her child out. This is anger at its height. She is so angry that the energy in her aura and body moves at its optimum light speed and accomplishes the impossible.

PINK Love

The only negative aspect of pink is if the color surrounds the head area. This implies that the person is ruled by their heart. They have difficulties being rational. This is called not living in reality. I have observed this color in many of my clients and find that person having great difficulties in relationships and accomplishing their life's work.

ORANGE Great Energy

This color gives energy and is associated with optimism. You may see blotches or streaks of orange in the auric field or in the body. If I am feeling low in energy, I will put on something orange or red to give me a boost.

WHITE Self-Confident

When a great deal of white is seen in the aura in and around the body, you will know that this person is quite clear and very positive. They are aware of who they are and where they are going. Sometimes you will see just a ring of white around the head area, like a halo.

GOLD Highly Advanced

An unusual color. Many have seen this color over the heads of great leaders, president's priests, rabbis, ministers, psychics and many others.

MAROON Moodiness

When you see this color, it represents a melancholy or moodiness in the personality. The person is discontent most of the time. Sometimes people will wear a maroon shirt or blouse a great deal of the time and don't understand why they are so attracted to that color. Because they are feeling so melancholy and a bit depressed it is the only color they feel comfortable wearing.

BROWN Disease

This color can be seen in various parts of the body. You might only see it surrounding a vital organ, such as the liver. You will know then that there is a problem with the subject's liver. We have a choice when this color is present! To heal ourselves either through our own efforts or through medical means.

BLACK Death

It is rare that you will see the subject's death. It usually stands for the death of a situation, a job, a relationship or even the death of the way the person relates to themselves. Many psychics interpret this black color as the impending death of the client. I have not found that to be true. At

What Is The Aura?

times I have been able to see the long distant future for that person and only then do I know that death is possibly out there. I will always direct that person to his or her physician.

Story of the Black Screen

While doing a reading for a lady in Sante Fe, New Mexico, in 1977, a strange thing occurred. Half way through she asked about her husband. I repeated his first name five times and wrote it down on a pad of paper. After being silent for several long minutes and seeing absolutely nothing but blackness, I opened my eyes and told the lady that I had to stop the reading. I returned her money against her wishes. My secretary, who was a nurse, became quite disturbed and thought I should rest awhile before going on to my next client. I followed her instructions and began again within 20 minutes. There were no problems with the following three clients.

Several weeks later, I received a call from a woman in New Mexico. She said, "Annette, I am so sorry that I haven't called before this, but when you hear what I have to say, you will understand. Annette, are you sitting down?"

I replied, "Yes, I am. What is wrong?" She went on, "Do you remember my reading and how you kept repeating my husbands first name and saw nothing but black when I asked about his health and future?" I acknowledged her question.

"Well, two nights, after you did the reading, my husband, Dr. D. dropped dead at the hospital while walking down the hallway! We ordered an autopsy and they found his body riddled with cancer. My husband never had any pain or any indication that he had cancer." I was speechless as she went on. "Thank you, Annette, for not telling me. I don't think I could have survived the knowing until it occurred. You are a talented and beautiful lady."

Responsibility

There is always the responsibility of reading the aura or a person, especially with regard to the persons physical conditions. You may offer advice; you may speak of methods that you know or have heard about that the individual may wish to explore, but you cannot legally diagnose or prescribe medicines!

My practice involves a great deal of diagnosing conditions in the body, mind and soul. If there are problems with the body or the mind, I always advise the client to see their physician or psychologist. Many times the physician or psychiatrist/ psychologist will send me their patients. By doing a reading and putting it on tape, which I do with all my readings, the patient and doctor will be able to use the tape as a guide line. We have had many complicated problems solved by this manner.

Strengthening and Protecting Your Aura

If you are unaware of how outside forces can affect you, you can end up with weaknesses in your own energy system. These weaknesses may begin to manifest an actual physical illness or mental/emotional imbalances in your life. Your energy system is being imposed and impinged upon every single day and unless you begin to recognize this phenomenon and work to protect yourself from unwanted intrusions, you may find your life becoming more complicated.

Everyone has had experiences in which our energies were affected by outside forces. Extraneous sounds, electrical and heat sounds occur frequently. Other individuals invade your energies as well. Has anyone tried to make you buy something or participate in an activity when you really did not want to? Have you felt drained after talking to a friend or some individual? All of these are intrusions upon your energy field.

What Is The Aura?

The key to protecting your energies lies with the aura. If you build up a strong and vibrant aura, negative, draining and unbalanced energies are thwarted.

How do you maintain a healthy aura?

It is not difficult, proper diet, exercise and fresh air are strengthening to the entire auric field, as well as using the *White Light*. Sunlight, exercise, fresh air is extremely vitalizing to the aura. Keeping the bowels clean assists in keeping the aura resilient. Meditation is strengthening and protective. Music is very good to balance and strength, such as classical or soft melodies.

Smudging

When I feel that a negative energy has bombarded my body or office I always get out my sage smudge sticks. Smudging in the native American tradition is common, it is the practice of using the smoke and fragrances of various herbs to cleanse the auric field or the environment. Within moments you will begin to feel the heaviness disappear. You can buy the smudge sticks at a native American store, get a dish and light the smudge stick till it begins to smoke. Cover yourself with your *White Light*. If you are doing a room, start in the center of the room and put the stick near the floor allowing the smoke to go up to the ceiling, then move to each corner of the room and allow the smoke to go from the floor to the ceiling. Open the windows and say outloud, "Out negative energies, out you go!" Don't forget the closets.

If you are smudging yourself, allow the smoke to start at your feet and move it around your auric field, till you feel comfortable. When you are smudging someone else, have them face you and start at the feet going up and around the front of the body, then move in back and do the same process.

Use of Crystals To Enhance the Aura

Your aura is extremely affected by your emotional and mental states. If you have continued stress, emotional trauma, mental disorders or imbalances, worry upheavals, fear and other negative emotions and attitudes these will weaken the auric field. You will begin to feel tired, listless and physical problems will begin to manifest themselves.

Another tool for protecting and strengthening the aura is a quartz crystal or stone. The electrical energy inherent within a crystal will amplify and strengthen the auric field. A good test is to have someone measure your aura *without* a crystal in your hand and then with one in your hand. Even a small, one-inch quartz crystal will increase the auric field by as much as three to four feet.

Crystal Experiment

Marcel Vogel, a noted scientist and visionary conducted an experiment before an audience of 300 people in 1979. Marcel was an expert with crystals and had cleared a large quartz crystal for this experiment where he would send my consciousness to the planet Mars. Outside of a witch entering the theater and calling out a death cry that put Marcel into a catatonic state for five minutes, the experiment was quite successful. My mind traveled faster than I had ever experienced and immediately found myself surveying the outer and inner ridges of Mars. All of my observations were confirmed when the Hubbell space craft returned to earth with pictures two years later.

Chapter 9

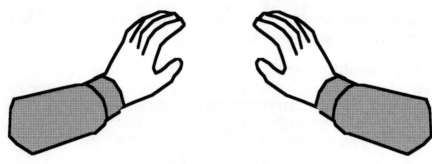

Your Aura
or
Electromagnetic Field

We now know that all human beings have an electromagnetic field of incredibly high frequency and low voltage. When we are feeling negative, it produces a negative field, and when we are feeling positive, it produces a positive field. This may be why people drink alcohol together-to release the positive "good fellowship field" among them. Thus far, we don't know very much about these ultra, ultra short-wave phenomena.

Have you ever walked into a room and felt overwhelmed by someone's love? Or have you met someone for the first time and knew instantly that you liked her? Perhaps you have been in a meeting and just knew that the stranger across the table could not be trusted though you just met him. Think about an immediate reaction you had about a person and write it down here.

Experience:

_____

_____

_____

_____

_____

_____

Anyone can feel his or her own auric field.
However it is most important to be in a relaxed state to do this.

Inner Guide

The following visualization script is intended to guide you through the process. You may want to have a partner read it to you or prerecord it yourself. Let's begin with the Meditation Process that we learned back in the first section then continue with the following.

Your Aura

On your blank, white movie screen picture yourself in a beautiful place. It might be a room or somewhere in nature. Wherever it is, allow the beautiful environment to form around you.

> *See it in your mind's eye.*
> *Feel the experience of being there.*
> *Look around you and take it all in.*

Our own wisdom lies hidden within.

Allow an image to appear before you. This might be a person, animal, or object. We will call it a guide.

Observe the guide and notice its appearance in detail. Experience its presence. Remember what it looks like.

This is your inner guide. The wonderful wisdom within you that is being personified or embodied through imagery.

Let your guide speak to you. Ask its name and why it has appeared.   (Pause)

Ask your guide for advice on a particular subject.

Thank your guide and release it back into the beautiful environment. Slowly let the environment fade and say good-bye, knowing that you can come back whenever you wish. Remember everything that you experienced.

Feel yourself coming back into the room again and into your body. Feel your body lying on the floor. See the blank movie screen up in front of your eyes.

Close your hands and make a fist, this will circulate all the white positive energy through your body.

Visualize your White Light and take in your three deep breaths. Breathe in through your nose and exhale through your mouth.

Breathe in, bringing the White Light in through the top of your head. Exhale.

Breathe in and bring the White Light down your body. Exhale

Breathe in one more time and feel the White Light circulating around your body.

Quickly exhale through your mouth, then return to regular breathing.

Slowly open your eyes and very slowly sit up. Do not talk. Write down everything that you experienced. If you feel dizzy after any meditation or visualization, close your eyes and take another few deep breaths and tell yourself to come straight back into your body.

Write out your conversation with your guide. You may want to do this as a right/left hand dialogue. Let your guide speak with your sub-dominant hand and respond with your dominant hand. Writing with the sub-dominant hand is optional in this exercise.

Your Aura

Meditation Journal

Meditation **Day** _____ **Time** _____

_____
_____
_____
_____
_____
_____
_____
_____
_____
_____
_____
_____
_____
_____
_____
_____
_____
_____
_____
_____
_____
_____
_____
_____
_____
_____
_____
_____
_____
_____
_____
_____

Your Aura

Size & Temperature

The size of the aura or electromagnetic field will differ according to how they are feeling at that given moment. You will begin to notice that when you are trying to feel someone else's aura, the intensity will differ from place to place.

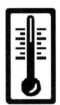

There can be a temperature change from one area of the aura to another. This could represent an imbalance somewhere in the body. Reading the aura and the temperature can be a great diagnostic tool, especially combined with dowsing rods. If we can become aware of an imbalance before other warning systems set into place, it is quite possible to prevent medical treatment in the earliest stages. Most often, if the aura is warm, there will be a cool spot where the imbalance is located.

When we ingest chemicals it will change the aura. Alcohol makes the aura porous. It looks like a sponge. The alcohol begins to depress the central nervous system, acting as an anesthetic. The person cannot tell how much negativity is being absorbed into their system.

Extremely sensitive people can get a "hangover" from very little alcohol. I am one of those people. One and a half drinks and I feel as if I have consumed five. The next morning, there's a pounding headache and my body aches from the alcohol. It just isn't fun!

What Does the Aura Tell Us?

The aura or electromagnetic field will tell us a great deal about a person even before we have any other information. Have you noticed that when you walk into a room and someone you have never met has his or her back to you, without any hesitation you get certain "vibes or feelings" about that person. Without thinking, your first response is, "I think I would like to know this person," or "I don't think I'll like that person." You are receiving information from the person's aura that is emanating who they are.

We do make judgments based on what is in the aura or electromagnetic field even before we are conscious of what is happening.

If you are receiving negativity from someone, you can overcome this by sending positive thoughts. A thought that is gentle and soft is nourishing a person's highest self through their aura or electromagnetic field. When I encounter negative energy I send White Light, which is pure positive energy. If you respond in the same negative way, you're fueling the negative engines.

If you paid more attention to these first impressions, you could save much pain and anguish on your emotions. Experiencing a person's electromagnetic field or aura is part of the communicative process. We then blend it with our logical, conscious understanding.

One of the ways to really experience a person's aura is to hug them. When you hug someone, you are totally within his or her auric field. Not only will you pick up feelings from that person, but they too will feel your energy. A hug is a wonderful healing device, and a great pick-me-up for when you're down.

I recommend four hugs a day and perhaps it could keep the doctor away.

Places and objects also have an electromagnetic field or aura around them. As we move along in our development, we will be working with objects and learning how we can pick up information about their owners. That process is called psychometry.

Your Aura

Now, let's practice.

Exercise 5
Feeling your aura

✔❏ If you have not just completed the previous exercise then return to the previous chapter and do the meditation exercise.

✔❏ Place your hands in front of you about two feet apart, elbows bent, hands relaxed, and have your palms facing one another.

✔❏ Begin to slowly move them toward one another. You might try closing your eyes for easier concentration. At some point, while moving your hands together, you will begin to feel a resistance. At first it may be so subtle that you overlook it. With practice, you will become more sensitive to the resistance. The resistance will occur when the aura of one hand touches the aura of the other.

If you look at the distance between the hands and divide it by two, you will have an idea of how large your aura is. If you concentrate on sending energy to your hands by means of the *White Light*, you will be able to increase the density of the aura, thereby increasing the resistance.

The next step is to "see" your aura. Our next exercise will help you to do just that.

Exercise 6
Seeing your aura

✔❏ Get comfortable and sit in front of a clean mirror. The wall or background behind the mirror should be white or a light color. You can put a white sheet behind the mirror, while you are practicing your exercise. If you have not just completed the previous exercise then return to the previous chapter and do the meditation exercise.

✔❏ Before you begin to look in the mirror, I want you to take in three deep breaths while visualizing the *White Light*. After your three deep breaths, gently close your eyes. Now squeeze your eyes very tightly for a few minutes and open them. They will feel relaxed as will your other facial muscles. Do this several times.

✔❏ It's time to look in the mirror. Gaze several inches above your head and a foot behind you in the mirror. Allow your eyes to go out of focus as you follow the outline of your head and shoulders. **Continue to do this for about five minutes**. Gradually your peripheral vision will begin to perceive a thin, pulsating line of light emanating from your head and shoulders, perhaps a half inch wide.

I see it!

Can you see it? If so, start to move your head from side to side.

✔❑ Are you following the light? Now take in a deep breath, breathing in through your nose and exhaling slowly through your mouth. Did you see your aura expand?

✔❑ Now I want you to think of a very positive thought while keeping an eye on your aura. Did the aura change because of the thought?

Positive thoughts will help to expand your energy field. I call positive thoughts food for my electromagnetic system.

The colors will probably be light or opaque when you begin and if you continue to practice they will get stronger. Do not become discouraged on the first couple of tries. It just requires practice.

Now that you have experienced your own aura, it is time to read someone else's.

Exercise 7
Aura gazing

✔❑ Have one person sit with their back to a blank, preferably white wall. Have a light on in the room or some daylight. This person is to sit against the wall, not move, with closed eyes, and relaxed.

✔❑ The reader will sit directly in front of the subject against the wall, approximately two to three feet away. Get comfortable and set a timer for five minutes.

✔❑ Focus your eyes on the center of the subject's forehead. You can blink your eyes as many times as you wish but do not move your head. Continue to stare at the subject's forehead.

✔❑ When your timer goes off, look to the right of the person's head and stare a few moments. Then turn and look to the left of the person's head for a few moments. Now look at the top of their head.

✔❑ Remember what you saw and stop.

✔❑ Blink your eyes and rub them if you wish. Close your eyes and take in your three deep breaths, bringing in the *White Light* . Then talk to your partner and tell them what you saw. Write it down on the aura reading notes on the following page.

Your Aura

✔❑ Switch places after a few minutes and repeat the exercise.

You can practice this exercise while sitting on a bus, listening to a lecture or sermon, or even in a restaurant. You can play a game and see how long it takes for that person to turn around and look at you, for they will feel your energy. After a while you will begin to see many colors and shapes around the heads and bodies of other people.

Aura-gazing Observations

Observer _____   **Date** _____

Observation of subject

_____
_____
_____
_____
_____
_____
_____
_____
_____
_____
_____

Exercise 8
How to feel another person's aura

✔❑ To feel another person's aura or electromagnetic field, stand behind that person while he or she is sitting down. Place your hands, palms down, three to five inches away from their head.

✔❑ Move your hands around the head, noticing any slight changes. The aura appears to be the strongest around the head and shoulders, so it is easier to sense it in this location. This does not mean that you cannot feel it elsewhere, because you will be able to identify the aura as you practice in different parts of the body.

✔❑ Start by moving your hands apart as wide as you can spread your arms. Then move in, much the same way when you were feeling your own aura within your hands. You will begin to feel an invisible wall or resistance. **This is their auric field.**

60

Your Aura

Homework

Aura-gazing Observations

1. How To Feel Another Persons Aura

If you can, choose a partner to work with. Set a time and day in the next week when you will practice reading each other's aura or electromagnetic field. Record your observations.

Observer _____ **Subject** _____ **Date** _____

_____
_____
_____
_____
_____
_____
_____
_____

2. Seeing Your Own Aura

If you are working alone, practice seeing your own aura in the mirror. You can practice this as many times as you like. **Remember only five minutes at a time.** The more you practice the easier it will be to see the electromagnetic energy coming from your body.

Observer _____ **Date** _____

Observation of subject

_____
_____
_____
_____
_____
_____
_____

Chapter 10

Day-dreaming & Dreams

"The Windows of Our Mind"

"Hold fast to dreams, for if dreams die, life is a broken winged bird that cannot fly." ***Langston Hughes***

In developing our psychic skills we need the ability to alter our consciousness at will. Whether you realize it or not, you are already operating in altered states of consciousness.

Consciousness is described as having all your mental faculties fully active. Anything other than this is a different, or altered, state of consciousness, such as night dreaming, daydreaming, absentmindedness, trance, hypnotic states, and meditation.

Daydreaming

When you are driving your car, doing dishes, staring out a window, or mowing the lawn you often let your mind "wander." Where does it go? It doesn't go anywhere, you shift from drive, or focus, gear to neutral, or daydreaming, gear. You are simply focusing on something other than what you were doing.

When we daydream you are removing yourself from your immediate environment and placing yourself in a different reality. It is not simply an escape from reality: it serves a vital function by helping to keep the outer self and inner self in balance.

By daydreaming you are providing an opportunity to visualize the way you want your future to be. How many times have you had a mental conversation with someone you were going to see? You find yourself going over the dialogue a number of times, changing the outcome so that by the time you have the actual conversation, you will be prepared for whatever the other person says. You are rehearsing a script.

Daydreams can be wish fulfilling, like a woman imagining a date with Kevin Costner or Robert Redford, or a man with Madonna or Demi Moore. When we desire something that is unattainable, daydreaming can provide a way to fulfill that desire. Our daydreaming can compensate for what you lack in your life, making you feel less deprived.

When we daydream about something that is attainable, it is called visualization. The ability to visualize brings you one step closer to getting what you want. We can do this by focusing our attention on the goal and then by directing mental energy toward it. The next step is to take the action necessary to make the goal a reality. Most of us fall short in focusing, not in acting. It is most important to have a clear picture or idea.

Day-dreaming & Dreams

We are going to learn how to develop the imagination, to create clear and detailed mental images. By paying close attention to your daydreams and directing them toward your goals, your visualization skills will improve. This in turn will train your psychic skills. With the newfound ability to use directed and powerful visualization, you can enhance your creativity, increase your energy level and maximize your concentration. You can raise your self esteem and eliminate bad habits. Any area of your life you feel needs help can be helped through the art of visualization.

Dreams

Your dreams have more to do with our waking reality than most of us give them credit for. Dreams have much to tell us about our unconscious behavior patterns, the way we view the world, and how we relate to others. Maybe you have had a recurring dream or one that was significant. Relate that dream here. I suggest that you buy a journal to record all your significant dreams.

Your Dream:

_____
_____
_____
_____
_____
_____
_____
_____
_____
_____
_____
_____
_____
_____
_____
_____
_____
_____
_____

Freud

With the turn of the century, the systematic and thorough dream analyses made by Freud began to permanently alter the way people thought of their dreams, as well as themselves. Drawing on his own dreams and those of his patients, Freud viewed the perplexing visions of the dreamer as "the royal road to the unconscious," a pathway to the world of long-buried impulses and conflicts lurking beneath consciousness. The strange creatures and puzzling events in our dreams, Freud argued, were symbols of desires too frightening for conscious thought; dreams were mechanisms by which we attempted to fulfill desires in carefully disguised form. Freud, like the Greeks, thought that dreams had therapeutic value. But while the Greeks saw them as a way to physical healing, Freud used them to treat emotional disorders.

Freud's ideas did much to revive the practice of dream interpretation and gave it scientific respectability. Like the ancients, he believed that dreams carried meaning, but he looked for that meaning in a dialogue between doctor and dreamer, in which the dreamer was encouraged to link conscious thoughts about dreams to deeper, hidden impulses and memories.

Day-dreaming & Dreams

Jung

Jung, Freud's eminent disciple-turned-critic, believed that sexuality was only one of several themes that emerged in most people's dreams, and that dreams served to reveal rather than to disguise the unconscious. "So flower like, is (the dream) in its candor and veracity," he wrote, "that it makes us blush for the deceitfulness of our lives."

Interestingly enough, neither Jung nor Freud completely ruled out the possibility that at least some dreams might bear messages from the outside. While Freud dismissed precognitive dreams as "quite out of the question," Jung surmised that one might dream of a future event as one of a number of probabilities. Jung also wrote that telepathy "undoubtedly exists."

Scientific investigation of telepathy and other paranormal experiences had begun shortly before Freud started his work. The British Society for Psychical Research members in 1882 uncovered 149 instances in which telepathic messages seemed to have been received in dreams; more than half concerned the death of someone known to the dreamer. After sending out questionnaires to 5,000 people, the replies satisfied the society that something more than chance had been at work.

Dreams & Your Health

Dr. Kasatkin, a Soviet scientist and medical doctor is a leading Russian professor of neuropathology at the famed Pavlov Institute of Physiology in St. Petersburg. He has spent 40 years analyzing more than 24,000 dreams and states that it is easy to distinguish between normal dreams and those that indicate a serious health problem.

The doctor claims that your dreams reveal your health. Amazingly, they can warn you about illness months before any physical symptoms show up. Dr. Kasatkin feels that dreams are neither random coincidences nor examples of dream-sleep precognition. Instead, he firmly believes that they are a part of significant cerebral pattern. He also states that some dreams can save your life.

The Strangling Python

A young student in St. Petersburg was experiencing a recurring nightmare where his body was immobilized by a strangling python. Finally, he became ill and sought medical help. The doctor he consulted could not find any problems. About a year later, the student developed a serious spinal tumor that threatened to leave his body completely paralyzed.

Crushed to Death

In another case, a woman dreamed over and over again of being crushed by earth until she was barely able to breath. Two months later she was diagnosed as having tuberculosis.

The Dream Band

The doctor also believes that the brain has the ability to sense illness and to provide dream-encoded warnings long before recognizable symptoms appear. He has theorized about what he calls the dream band, the brain's outer layer of active cells, register "the minute deviation from normal conditions" in the body. Especially at night when distractions are at a minimum, one might pick up minute physiological changes that would otherwise go unnoticed.

It has been Dr. Kasatkin's belief that a thorough understanding of and familiarity with such dreams might constitute a potentially valuable tool for diagnosis. The doctor has collected thousands of cases in which, he contends, he could detect certain predictive patterns.

Occasionally nightmares should be ignored, but when nightmares recur they should be taken as warnings. Not every bad dream is health related but some troublesome dreams may result from emotional upset, overeating, or drinking too much alcohol.

The moment a person dreams about his body and the dream has some unpleasantness, it can mean trouble. You don't have to be alarmed about a possible serious illness until you have had the same dream at least several times over a period of weeks.

Recurring Dream

One of the more recent cases Dr. Kasatkin worked with was that of a 58 year old office worker who had a recurring dream about being wounded in battle. In each dream he would be wounded in the right side. Dr. Kasatkin told the patient to have his liver checked out. The patient followed his advice and went for an examination, but nothing was found. Meanwhile, he continued to have the same dream.

The doctor urged the patient to return for another liver examination. He finally did and the tests revealed the patient had developed liver cancer. His dreams clearly warned he was going to have serious problems with his liver—three full months before the doctors were able to find anything wrong. Because his cancer was diagnosed so early, he is alive and well today.

The Warning Period

The warning period given by dreams varies with the illness. Cancer signals show up in dreams several months to half a year before the disease is usually diagnosed. Heart disease warnings may appear in dreams three months ahead of time.

On the other hand, quick-striking illnesses such as a cold or flu may reveal themselves in dreams two or three days in advance. If you have pleasant dreams, or if you don't remember your dreams, these are good signs. They mean you are in good health.

Other Doctors' Opinions

Dr. Henri F. Ellenberger, emeritus professor of Psychiatry at the University of Montreal, Canada, declared,

"Dreams can definitely be used to predict physical problems. If people would pay more attention to dreams and learn to interpret them they might be able to head off illness."

Some dreams are precognitive and point to future directions our lives may take. They can also provide valuable information about probable outcomes of current situations and show us our relationships and how we are handling them. If our doctors were skilled in recognizing and interpreting such dreams, Kasatkin has contended, they might be able to detect serious illnesses at an early and treatable stage.

Day-dreaming & Dreams

How to Help Ourselves

To gain consciousness of our dreams for their value and energy, we must begin to remember them and then record them. Many people say they don't dream or can't remember their dreams. If you want to remember your dreams, you can train yourself to do so. Here are some simple techniques for dream recall in Exercise 9.

Exercise 9
Remembering your dreams

✔❑ Practice auto-suggestion before going to sleep. As you drift off to sleep, say to yourself: "I am going to remember my dreams when I wake up."

✔❑ Now let yourself float off to dream land. Don't worry about whether you will succeed or not. Just relax and go to sleep. If you don't recall your dreams at first, continue this auto-suggestion every night until your dreams start coming through.

Planting Seeds (the wish to remember dreams) in the unconscious mind during that twilight zone between waking and sleeping can yield a rich harvest of consciously remembered dreams.

✔❑ Upon waking, review the dream before opening your eyes. Go over the dream in your mind's eye as soon as you awaken but before opening your eyes, remember as much as you can. It's as though you were playing back a movie. It helps to, "Fix" the dream in your memory by giving it a title.

✔❑ Focus on the highlights: Key people, objects, events, experiences, visual impressions, etc.

This review is a quick, condensed version of the dream, somewhat like the coming attractions for a feature length film. It is important that you do this before opening your eyes and becoming distracted by the outer world.

In this transition state between sleep and waking, there is greater access to the unconscious and to the dream world. If you get up at this point and start your regular activities before reviewing the dream, chances are good that the dream will vanish.

✔❑ You can set the alarm clock to awaken you during the night. This will interrupt your dream. Write the dream down or talk into a voice-activated tape recorder.

Exercise 10
Documenting your dreams

✔❑ Write in the present tense or draw a picture or sketch of the dream in your journal or tape record it (to be transcribed later into your journal) or use a voice-activated recorder.

Day-dreaming & Dreams

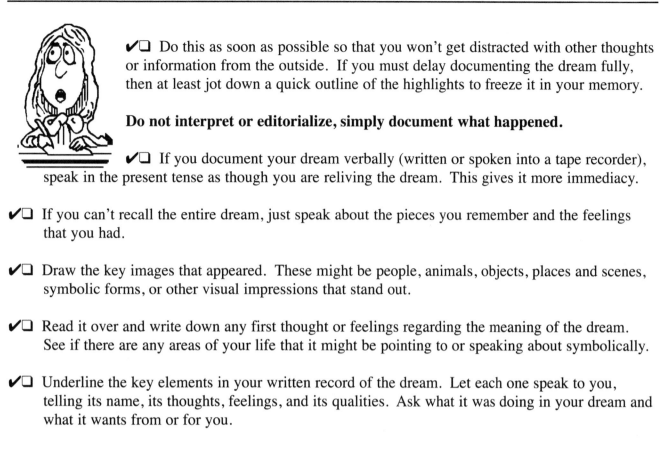

✔❑ Do this as soon as possible so that you won't get distracted with other thoughts or information from the outside. If you must delay documenting the dream fully, then at least jot down a quick outline of the highlights to freeze it in your memory.

Do not interpret or editorialize, simply document what happened.

✔❑ If you document your dream verbally (written or spoken into a tape recorder), speak in the present tense as though you are reliving the dream. This gives it more immediacy.

✔❑ If you can't recall the entire dream, just speak about the pieces you remember and the feelings that you had.

✔❑ Draw the key images that appeared. These might be people, animals, objects, places and scenes, symbolic forms, or other visual impressions that stand out.

✔❑ Read it over and write down any first thought or feelings regarding the meaning of the dream. See if there are any areas of your life that it might be pointing to or speaking about symbolically.

✔❑ Underline the key elements in your written record of the dream. Let each one speak to you, telling its name, its thoughts, feelings, and its qualities. Ask what it was doing in your dream and what it wants from or for you.

If the dream seems to be speaking about a specific issue in your life, then write further about it.

This exercise provides a tool for examining the symbolic forms and events in your dreams and relating these symbols to everyday life situations.

By learning to identifying with the elements, (getting inside them and speaking for them), you can gain a deeper understanding of how they represent those parts of yourself.

The story of the dream may indicate one issue in your life or one layer of experience. Your conversations with the parts might uncover still another level of meaning. When we begin to dig into our dreams it is like doing a geological survey, with many strata of symbolic messages dwelling under the surface of the dream plot.

When you have accumulated at least 10 to 13 dreams you can begin to look at them and re-read your notes. Up to this point you will only become confused. You will begin to see a pattern in the dreams and you will start to recognize your symbols.

Z Z Z Z Z Z *Night-night and have fun!*

Day-dreaming & Dreams

Understanding Your Own Symbols

To learn how to interpret our dreams we need to have our own set of symbols. What a train means to you, certainly means something different to me. We need to determine our own symbols, so that we can understand and identify our dreams.

Write out what these objects represent for you

Train _____
_____
_____

House _____
_____
_____

Water _____
_____
_____

Star _____
_____
_____

Trees _____
_____
_____

Red Car _____
_____
_____

Dog _____
_____
_____

Cat _____
_____
_____

Mother _____
_____
_____

Day-dreaming & Dreams

Father

Knife

Ship or boat

Bicycle

Flying

Letters

Telephone

Alarm Clock

Making Movies

Television

Horse

Moon

Day-dreaming & Dreams

Santa Claus

The Sun

Flowers

Wine

New Year

Flag

Spring

Summer

Autumn

Winter

Bridge

Snake

Day-dreaming & Dreams

Dream Journal

Day _____   **Time** _____

Dream:

_____
_____
_____
_____
_____
_____
_____
_____
_____
_____
_____
_____
_____
_____
_____
_____
_____
_____
_____
_____
_____
_____
_____
_____
_____
_____
_____
_____

Chapter 11

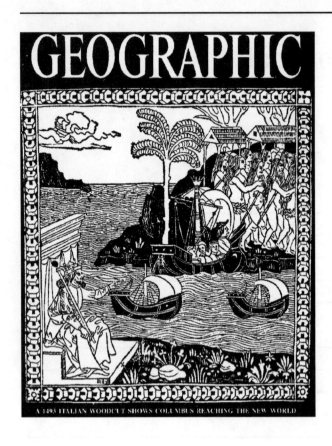

A 1493 ITALIAN WOODCUT SHOWS COLUMBUS REACHING THE NEW WORLD

Sending a Magazine Picture

The following visualization script is intended to guide you through the process. You may want to have a partner read it to you or pre-record it yourself.

Let's begin with the Meditation Process in Chapter 4 then continue with the following.

Visualization - Loved One

You are feeling very relaxed. Gently concentrate on seeing a blank, white movie screen in front of your closed eyes.

Think of someone that you love very much and have had wonderful times with. Maybe you laughed and cried together. Choose someone that means a great deal to you.

Form a picture of that person and put them on your large movie screen. See their face, their body, their hands. Look at the color of their hair and what kind of clothes they have on.

Now look around you. Are you at home, at the beach, in the car, where are you?

Remember everything that you are looking at.   (Pause)

It's time to experience and relive a joyful time the two of you had together. Enjoy the experience, relive it again. Be aware of all your emotions. Feel your love for him or her and that person's love for you.

Remember everything that you feel, see, hear, taste and touch.   (Pause)

Allow yourself to come back into the room and into your body. Feel your body lying on the floor.

Close your hands and make a fist. This will circulate all the positive energy through your body.

*Visualize your **White Light** and take in your three deep breaths. Breathe in through the nose and exhale through your mouth.*

Sending a Magazine Picture

*Breathe in, bringing the **White Light** in through the top of your head.   Exhale.*

*Breathe in and bring the **White Light** down your body.   Exhale*

*Breathe in one more time and feel the **White Light** circulating around your body.*

Quickly exhale through your mouth. Then return to regular breathing.

Slowly open your eyes and very slowly sit up. Do not talk and write down everything that you experienced. If you feel dizzy after any meditation or visualization close your eyes and take another few deep breaths and tell yourself to come straight back into your body.

Write down everything that you experienced during the meditation and visualization.

Meditation Journal

Day _____ **Time** _____

Meditation:

_____
_____
_____
_____
_____
_____
_____
_____
_____
_____
_____
_____
_____
_____
_____
_____
_____
_____
_____
_____
_____

Sending a Magazine Picture

Positive versus Negative Attitudes

Let's talk a little about your attitude. As you continue with your development, you will be able to image someone who needs emotional or physical assistance. You will be equipped to direct positive thought to that person and help them.

Negative Emotions   If you permit yourself to dwell upon negative emotions such as anger or resentment, or wish harm to an other human being, you may unwittingly bring unhappiness to that person. They will, at the very least, be negatively affected by you.

What Goes Out, Comes Back   All psychics realize the truth in the old adage claiming that whatever you give comes back to you tenfold. If you wish harm to another person your wish may come true, but you will be harmed as well. If you wish something good for an other person you will receive something good. Never expect your rewards to come from the person you have helped. They generally come from the most unexpected sources.

Asking   As you learn to develop your mind and your sixth sense, you will discover whatever you wish for comes to you. If you desire something, ask for it. State your wish out loud to a friend or family member, not expecting them to fulfill it. Be explicit. Remember, you get exactly what you ask for.

Success   You'll never meet a successful businessman who doesn't believe in himself. Successful people never permit themselves to consider the possibility of failure. They consciously use positive thought projection. I firmly believe that everything we experience in our outer existence is the direct result of our innermost thoughts, attitudes, and expectancies.

Expect Only Positive Results   Learn to expect positive results in your life and you will receive them. Maintain a conviction of success in your business dealings. Expect the best from other people. Know that you can meet any challenge.

Approach Life with a Positive Attitude   Keep your objectives in sight. Believe in your capabilities and relax. Don't struggle with life. This depletes your energies and hinders positive action. As you bring positive attitudes into your life, success will naturally follow. When you become frustrated by the inept or negative behavior of others, you maybe tempted to give them "a piece of your mind." Instead it would be far more beneficial to you and to them if you gave them "a piece of your positive attitude." By doing it this way, you will be showing them how to adjust their attitude. They will feel better and so will you.

Now, let's go on to our next exercise in sending a magazine picture.

Sending a Magazine Picture

> ## Exercise 11
> ## Sending a magazine picture
> ### This requires a partner

✔❏ You will need a magazine with pictures for the Sender and a blank piece of paper and drawing utensil for the Receiver.

✔❏ Sit on the floor or in chairs, with your backs to each other. Decide which person will be the Sender and which person will be the Receiver. Enter your names in the following recording sheet.

✔❏ The Sender will hold a magazine picture. The Receiver will have a blank piece of paper to draw on.

✔❏ Begin by both opening your hands and taking in three deep breaths, drawing in the *White Light*. This will help to clear the mind.

✔❏ **Sender** Pick up the picture and begin to concentrate on it. Look at all aspects of the picture. Really see it in your mind. If it is filled with emotion, feel the emotion in the picture. Keep looking and concentrating on the picture. It is most important that you understand clearly what you are looking at. Give feedback, be encouraging. Always be positive, do not speak with a negative tone. The more positive feelings they receive from you the quicker and easier they will see the whole picture that you are sending.

✔❏ **Receiver** Relax and bring up your blank screen. **Do not try** to think about anything and just let the pictures come up on your screen. If you are having trouble seeing, feeling, or knowing, take a few more deep breaths to relax yourself. Once you begin to see or feel something, draw it on your piece of paper no matter what it is. *Remember it is always those first feelings or pictures you see that are correct.*

If you can't draw, then write down the words of what you are experiencing. If you feel emotions write them down. Begin to verbalize to your partner what you are seeing. **Just let it come to you, do not try to see it.**

✔❏ **Do this exercise for 10 minutes and stop.** Close your hands, make a fist, and do your three deep breaths, always using the *White Light*.

✔❏ Turn and face each other and compare your experience with the magazine picture. Write down, on the following page, what was sent and what was received. Then switch places and repeat the exercise.

Sending a Magazine Picture

Picture in Magazine Recording Sheet

Sender's Name _____ **Date** _____

Picture Sent: (Photocopy and paste a miniature here or write a short description)

Receiver's Name _____ **Date** _____

Picture Sent: (Photocopy and paste a miniature here or write a short description)

Sending a Magazine Picture

Here are some examples from my previous students.

Sender

Receiver

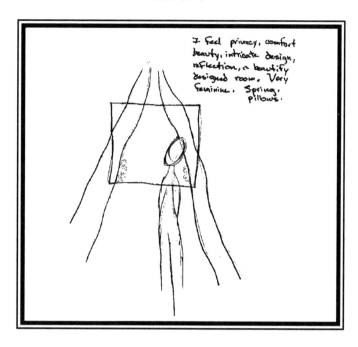

I feel privacy, comfort, beauty, intricate design, reflection, a beautify designed room. Very feminine. Spring, pillows.

Sender

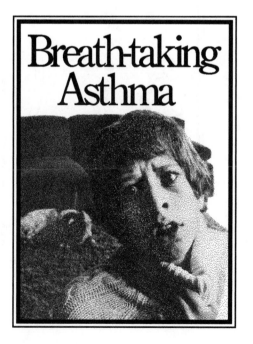

Receiver

"I feel as if there are midsection problems. Trouble with breathing, like Emphysema."
Shin Takeck,

Sending a Magazine Picture

Sender

Title of Picture: A Second Chance

Receiver

> I first saw a reddish blob. Then a picture of a lady in love appeared on my screen. Then a male. I had the feeling of a window and then a feeling of being in jail or prison.

Sender

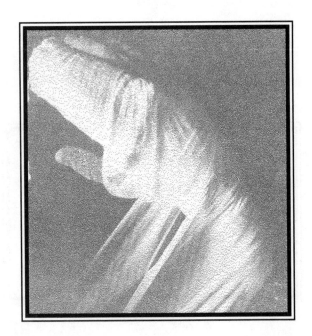

Receiver

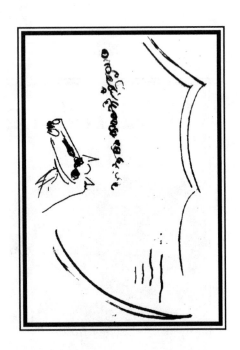

Sending a Magazine Picture

Homework

1. Choose a partner to work with. Set a time and day of the next week, where you will practice sending and receiving a magazine photo. Or, you may choose to close your eyes and flip through a magazine, stop and see if you can pick up what is on the page without looking. You can do this as many times as you wish. Just keep track of your successes.

2. Write down in your book, if you are to be the sender or the receiver and record your observations.

Sender's Name _____ **Date** _____

Picture Sent: (Photocopy and paste a miniature here or write a short description)

Receiver's Name _____

Picture Received: (Photocopy and paste a miniature here or write a short description)

Sending a Magazine Picture

Homework

Letters to Others

Sometimes letters contain important statements about the letter-writer's life. Your letters are worth keeping as a record of your life at a given point in time. A letter can also be an important tool in clarifying thoughts, feelings, and wishes about yourself. It can also be about the person to whom the letter is written.

Should You Mail All Letters?

Not all letters to others need to be sent. In some situations, a private letter written in your journal can help you understand and formulate your inner response to the other person in a relationship. In this way you can sort things out and perhaps become clearer about your feelings. Of course, you may decide to share the feelings face-to-face. In this instance, the private journal letter serves as a preparation ground for more direct and effective communication. You may even want to give a copy of all or part of the letter to the other individual.

Uses

This is a way of documenting your own personal history as you live it. It is also a tool for clarifying relationships and promoting better communication.

Letter

Write a letter to someone you have a problem with or a letter to yourself.

Dear _____   **Date** _____

_____
_____
_____
_____
_____
_____
_____
_____
_____
_____
_____
_____
_____
_____
_____
_____

Chapter 12

Helping Yourself

Power of a Smile

It costs nothing, but creates much. It enriches those who receive it, without impoverishing those who give it.

It happens in a flash, and the memory of it sometimes lasts forever.

No one is so rich that he can get along without it, and no one is so poor, but that he is richer for its benefits.

It creates happiness in the home, fosters goodwill in business, and is the countersign of friends.

It is rest to the weary, daylight to the discouraged, sunshine to the sad, and nature's best antidote for trouble.

Yet it cannot be bought, begged, borrowed or stolen, for it is something that is of no earthly good to anyone unless it is given away.   *unknown author*

Before we go on, I would like to talk to you about some old folk wisdom that urges you to smile and laugh your troubles away! Did you know that just the act of flexing facial muscles into the characteristic expressions of joy or other emotions can produce effects on the nervous system that normally go with those emotions?

Researchers feel that the mechanics of facial muscle movement are closely tied to the nervous system which controls our heart rate, breathing, and other vital involuntary functions. And laughter strengthens the immune system. It also causes the brain to release endorphins, chemicals that act in the body to help relieve pain.

Have you ever noticed yourself mimicking the expressions of those around you? If you have it may produce the same effects on the nervous system. This may be one of the reasons audiences react emotionally to the theater, why smiling faces at parties seem infectious and why smiling faces are successful in advertising. Children seem to be the most in touch with laughter, which is an expression of emotional well-being. They just laugh out of joy and happiness, not because anything is particularly hilarious or funny.

Lighten up! Be happy!

Helping Yourself

It's Not Easy to...

Apologize

Keep trying

Make the best of life

Shoulder a deserved blame

Recognize a silver lining

Begin over

Take advice

Face a sneer

Forgive and forget

Admit error

Be unselfish

Avoid mistakes

Think and then act

Be charitable

But It Always Pays!

Even a happy life cannot be without a measure of darkness. The word, "happy" would lose its meaning if it were not balanced by sadness.

A Laughing Exercise

Laughter is one of the best medicines that can be found for many physical or emotional problems. A good healthy laugh should begin from deep in the belly, but so many of us have been programmed to giggle or laugh quietly, rather than really laugh outloud. I am guilty of laughing loudly and frequently, but I also know that I am a very happy, well-adjusted person, who takes on many projects, and always completes them with great joy. I have been accused of making other people laugh with me, isn't that wonderful? You can do the same, it's so easy. I have come up with a little exercise that you can do in the morning to start your day.

✔❑ Begin each day by laughing for five minutes.

✔❑ Start with repeating Ha Ha Ha Ha. Feel the sound coming from your tummy, let it shake, rattle, and roll.

✔❑ I know this sounds silly but within a few minutes you will begin to start laughing at yourself.

✔❑ If anyone is within earshot they may come in and ask what you are laughing about. Believe me within a few minutes you will have them laughing as well. It is indeed infectious.

✔❑ Laughter will lighten all those heavy stresses or burdens you have been carrying around, making you feel wonderful, light, not so serious, and able to look at the world from a different perspective.

Remember we must learn to laugh at ourselves, lest we take ourselves too seriously.

Helping Yourself

✔❑ We are going to make three lists. First make a list of things you wish to eliminate from your life. Use the section following in the workbook.

Examples: Negative character traits, anxiety, cruelty, confusion, conflict, inferiority, or guilt. Include everything you can think of that impedes or restricts you.

Perhaps a relationship that no longer has any meaning or something that is detracting you from the kind of quality that you want in your life. Be honest in your evaluation. Make a sharp, clean cut from all things you have retained in your life that are unnecessary.

As you set definite goals in your life, you'll find you have little time for the busywork that previously filled your hours. Eliminate all that is mediocre in your life. You must eliminate the old before you will be able to receive the new. Remember, if you accept second best, you won't be able to achieve a true measure of success.

✔❑ Make a list of all the things you desire in your life. Use the section provided in the workbook.

Be specific. Remember...you get exactly what you ask for.

Read through your list of desires each day, concentrating on each entry, and believing with certainty that right action is bringing good things into your life.
- Learn to stop worrying about things.
- Learn to relax and expect life's joys and riches.
- Be ready to accept them.
- They will come as the natural result of positive attitudes.

✔❑ Make a list of things for which you are grateful. Use the section provided in the workbook. Be explicit. Read this list every day, or at least several times a week and say thank you. Your lists should be written in pencil. They will change continually. As you continue, you will find yourself needing to eliminate more and more from your life in preparation for new and better experiences.

Helping Yourself

Things To Eliminate

_____
_____
_____
_____
_____
_____
_____
_____
_____
_____

Things You Desire

_____
_____
_____
_____
_____
_____
_____
_____
_____
_____

Grateful For Eliminating

_____
_____
_____
_____
_____
_____
_____
_____
_____
_____

Grateful For Desiring

_____
_____
_____
_____
_____
_____
_____
_____
_____
_____

Chapter 13

Psychometry

"How dangerously one-sided we've become by ignoring our intuitive and instinctive side."
Carl Jung

Have you ever picked up an object and had an odd sensation? Maybe a feeling of warmth, love, hate, or just a queasiness in the pit of your stomach? You might not believe it, but those feelings were probably a good indication that the object that you picked up was associated with that very same emotion. Try to reflect on just such an experience. Write down the object and the emotions you experienced.

Object: _____

Experience:

_____

_____

_____

_____

_____

Each and every thing that we touch we leave with an invisible print-just as we do with our fingerprints. We cannot see them unless a detective comes along and dusts an area with a special powder and "viola" there are a bunch of fingerprints. Magic!

We have learned that we have an electromagnetic or aura print around our whole bodies, so why can't we leave an invisible print when we touch something? We call this type of reading *psychometry.*

Uses of Psychometry

Police work *I use psychometry exclusively when I am working on police cases. I use it when I am looking for a person (dead or alive) or the assailant.*

Clients *When a client comes in for a reading and wants me to tell him or her about a husband, wife, child, co-worker, boss, or friend, I ask the client to bring along a photo so that I can psychometrize the picture. I am picking up feelings and pictures from the photograph. The photo holds an image of our electromagnetic field or aura.*

African Massai

The African Massai will not let you take their photo for fear that you will be taking away their spirit. They are very cognizant of the energy field that envelopes the body. The African Massai live in survival mode every day.

Psychometry

A week before we arrived in Africa, two British tourists were stabbed by several Massai warriors. They had asked to take a tall, handsome African's picture and he refused. But the Englishmen laughed and took their photographs anyway; they were killed instantly. In Africa, the law states that you do not photograph the Massai.

Your Own Sensations

While doing the exercises in psychometry, you will begin to become aware of certain feelings or sensations that you have not paid attention to before. These sensations could be:

- Butterflies in your stomach
- A feeling deep inside your stomach
- Feeling in your bones
- Prickling of your thumbs
- Sensation on the end of your nose
- Goose bumps
- Eyes fluttering
- Hot sensation
- Cold sensation
- Surges of energy running through your body
- Lightheadedness or blood pressure falling
- Ears ringing

Before we begin our exercise in psychometry, we are going to experience a new way of progressively relaxing our muscles, followed by our Meditation and regression visualization.

(The following visualization script is intended to guide you through the process. You may want to have a partner read it to you or pre-record it yourself.)

Learning to Progressively Relax Our Muscles

Progressive Relaxation was introduced in the 1930s in Chicago by Edmund Jacobson, who was working as a researcher in clinical physiology. This is a simple but very effective means of producing total muscular relaxation.

This method is an exercise in feedback learning, where we learn the *feeling* of total relaxation in all the muscle groups in order that you may learn to switch the state on and off at will. The exercises can take up to 10 minutes to go through, but after the technique has been learned you can shorten it to three minutes and finally down to about 20 seconds.

✔❑ Either seat yourself in a comfortable arm chair or lay flat on the floor or on a bed. Each of your main groups of muscles will be successively tensed then relaxed several times for between two and five seconds in the following order.

✔❑ Have a partner read the following or tape it ahead of time.

Reminiscing

Allow yourself to relax in a chair or lying down. Arms facing upward. Move your feet apart, so that the thighs are not touching.

Point your toes and curl them gently for a couple of seconds. Relax and repeat three times.

Psychometry

Point the toes of both feet and curl them gently inward for two seconds-you don't want to cause a cramp. Relax and repeat three times.

Now tense the muscles in your calf for five seconds. Relax. Repeat three times.
Now tense the upper thighs for five seconds. Relax for five seconds. Repeat three times.

Tense your stomach muscles as though you were about to have someone punch you in the stomach. Hold for five seconds. Relax for five seconds. Repeat three times.

Take a deep breath, hold it and pull your shoulder blades back to the floor or chair. Hold for five seconds. Let the breath out, through your mouth and relax for five seconds. Repeat three times.

Clench the fist of your dominant hand (the hand you write with) tightly for five seconds. Now relax it for five seconds. Repeat three times.

Tense the biceps of this dominant arm for five seconds. Again relax for five seconds. Repeat three times.

Go to your other fist and clench it for five seconds and relax it for five seconds. Repeat three times. Tense the biceps of this other arm the same way, and repeat three times.

Pull your chin down to your chest, but do not let it touch your chest. You do this by tensing the neck muscles. Do this for five seconds, then relax for five seconds. Repeat three times.

Pull the corners of your mouth back toward your ears. This will tense the muscles in your lower cheeks and jaws for five seconds. Then relax for five seconds. Repeat three times.

Wrinkle your nose up, tensing the muscles in your nose and upper cheeks for five seconds. Relax for five seconds. Repeat three times.

You can either raise your eyebrows or frown hard, which will tense the muscles in your forehead for five seconds. Relax for five seconds. Repeat three times.

Your body is feeling totally relaxed and you have learned how to make your muscles do what you want. It is very important to feel the state of relaxation that follows the tension.

*Your whole body is feeling totally relaxed. Take in your three deep breaths. Breathe in deeply through your nose and see your **White Light** coming down through the top of your head. Exhale through your mouth.*

*Take in another deep breath and feel the **White Light** move down your body. Exhale.*
*Breathe in one more time very deeply and feel the **White Light** go out your feet, encircling your entire body. Exhale.*

*Breathe normally and gently visualize a blank movie screen in front of your closed eyes. Take in a deep breath, feeling yourself surrounded by your **White Light** bubble and exhale.*

See yourself on the screen as seven years old. Where are you? (pause) What are you doing? (pause) What do you have on? (pause) . What colors are you wearing? (pause)

Remember everything you experienced. (pause) Let's go back a little further to five years old.

Psychometry

(pause)   Where are you now? (pause)   What are you doing? (pause)

Reach out to someone you love. (pause)   Look at them. (pause)   How do they look? (pause).   What do they have on? (pause)   What colors are they wearing? (pause)   Remember everything you experienced. (pause)

Now let's go back even further. Back, back to your mother's womb. What's it like in there? (pause) Are you comfortable? (pause)   Is it warm or cold? (pause) Are you crowded or is there plenty of space for you.? (pause) What kind of sensations are you feeling? (pause)

Remember everything you experienced. (pause)

I want you to go back even further now.

Let's step back over into another time. Just gently let the picture come to you.   Watch the pictures on your screen and remember them.   [Pause for two minutes]

Now come back to the age you are now, in this life. Feel yourself lying on the floor. You are feeling very rested and relaxed. This has been a pleasant experience for you.

*Close your hands and make a fist. Breathe in deeply, see your **White Light** and exhale. Breathe in again and exhale.*

One last time, breathe in deeply and hold it, hold it, and exhale quickly through your mouth. Resume your regular breathing and slowly open your eyes.

✔❑ Write down everything you experienced on your journey back into time.

Seeing Yourself at Seven Years Old

Tell me where you were?

_____

Describe what you were doing?

_____

_____

What did you wear and what colors were the clothes?

_____

_____

Seeing Yourself at Five Years Old

Tell me where you were?

_____

Describe what you were doing?

_____

Who did you reach out to love?

Psychometry

How did they look-what kind and color of clothes were they wearing?

Back into Your Mother's Womb

Describe how you felt there.

Describe what it was like there.

Describe your level of comfort.

Was it warm or cold?

Were you crowded or was there plenty of space for you?

Back into Another Time

Describe where you went. Perhaps another century?

What kind of clothes were you wearing? Describe.

What kind of surroundings were you in? Landscape, buildings, etc.

What kind of utensils or tools did you use? Describe.

Could you smell, taste, or hear different things? Describe.

Psychometry

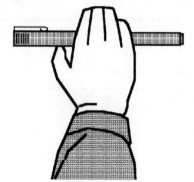

Now, let's try our hand at reading an object which we call psychometry.

✔❑ We are going to take different objects such as:

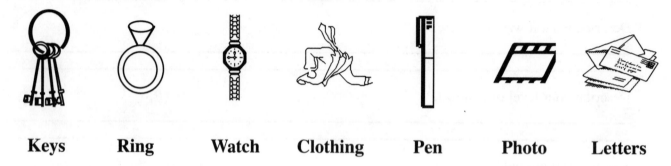

Keys   **Ring**   **Watch**   **Clothing**   **Pen**   **Photo**   **Letters**

✔❑ If you are doing this in a class setting, have one person go into another room and have each person bring one or more objects to be placed in a basket, one at a time. Do not let anyone see what is being put into the basket.

✔❑ If you are doing this exercise alone with someone, the reader will just take the object and hold it in his or her hands.

✔❑ Have your reader sit in the middle of the circle with closed eyes, reach into the basket, and choose one object. (Reader: take your time and choose an object that feels perhaps warm or good to you.)

✔❑ Hold the object up in the air.

✔❑ The person it belongs to will raise their hand, but will not speak. Remember only the teacher, leader, or if it is only two people, the owner will speak.

✔❑ **Reader** put the object down on the floor or in your lap and take in your three deep breaths, bringing in the *White Light*. Bring up your blank white screen.

✔❑ **Leader, teacher or owner** will speak. "You will be able to pick up on your screen, pictures and feelings from these objects and relay to us what you are experiencing."

✔❑ Now pick up the object, keep your eyes closed, and relax.

✔❑ Let the thoughts and pictures come to you. Begin to talk and tell what you are experiencing.

✔❑ The person whom the object belongs to will nod his or her head in response to your findings.

Psychometry

Normally you will pick up the information about the owner, from the object. However it has been my experience that some students pick up on the former owner or possibly the maker of the object.

✔❏ Hold the object in your hands and turn it around as much as you wish.

✔❏ If you do not begin to see, feel, know, sense, or smell anything, then put the object up to the center of your forehead.

✔❏ Take in a few more deep breaths. Take your time, relax, and have fun.

✔❏ Some questions that can be posed to the reader: What are you seeing? Can you tell us about the person to whom the object belongs? What are you feeling? Can you go to the home of the person this object belongs to and tell us what you see, feel, hear, smell, or taste?

✔❏ **Only do this exercise for 10 minutes or shorter** if the reader appears to be frustrated, tired, or anxious.

✔❏ **Teacher or leader** tell the reader to put down the object, make a fist, take in three deep breaths, and cover themselves with the beautiful *White Light* . On the third breath exhale quickly and open the hands. Open the eyes and give the reader instant feedback. Remember the reader may have been seeing things in a symbolic way, so it is most important to talk about what they saw, felt, or thought about the situation.

We learn through feedback, which I feel is one of the most important aspects of becoming a good reader.

An Example of a Psychometry Reading

"We were doing exercises in psychometry and I was amazed at some of the readings people were coming up with. Finally it was my turn and I sat down in front of Annette, closed my eyes and dipped my hand into the box to retrieve one of the objects belonging to one of the students in the class. I held the object up, my eyes closed all the time, and suddenly as I put my hands into my lap and began to concentrate, my hand and arm began to cramp and twist. It was visible to the class and frankly had me a little scared. I was not prepared for this sort of effect-an actual physical reaction.

"Annette questioned me about the woman [whom the object belonged to], whether the cramp was physical or mental-it was emotional I said. This woman is afraid of surgery. And when Annette asked what else I could say about her, what characteristic could I read, I answered 'determined.' That popped into my head.

"Later I found that I had been reading my friend Eva, who had been typing furiously and writing the night before. Eva is not happy with her electric typewriter and uses her very old manual typewriter usually. Evidently she had a session of trying to work with the electric typewriter and somehow ended with a very cramped arm.

"Writing is a very emotional and frustrating procedure for Eva, but if one were to choose one word to describe her in all her endeavors 'determined' would be the word of choice." Stella Savage

Psychometry

Homework

Choose a partner to work with. Ask your partner to bring a picture, watch, or ring of someone and see what information you can pick up. Your partner can give you feedback. Set a time and day next week, when you will practice your psychometry. You can do this as often as you wish. Just keep track of your successes. Write down in your book if you are to be the sender or the receiver and record your observations.

Date _____ Time _____

Object	Receiver	Observations

Chapter 14

Dowsing

Up to this point in our exercises we have been dealing directly with our right brain. Learning to dowse is another process of using our total mind. Here we are going to keep a fixed picture in our conscious mind of the object or commodity that we are searching for and at the same time allow our right brain, the subconscious mind, to be free and open to all pictures, thoughts, feelings, smells, and sounds that come onto our blank white screen.

Dowsing is another step towards your education in reading a human being. We have experienced the sending of emotions from one person to another whereby we used both sides of the brain. The sender was re- experiencing an emotional scene that was familiar and part of their conscious waking mind. The emotion was then sent immediately to the subconscious mind, thus the pictures and thoughts were being transmitted simultaneously. As the receiver you were able to pick up those feelings in your subconscious mind, whereby they were then transmitted to your conscious mind. This allowed you to write out and verbally give the sender feedback on the emotions you were receiving.

Now you will be cross-referencing information again by practicing the dowsing exercises. You will discover that you can pick up thoughts in your subconscious, visualize them through your conscious mind, and in turn they will send a message to your muscles and cause the dowsing rods to move.

Dowsing, or Radesthesia, is the method and art of locating hidden things, such as, underground water, gold, sunken ships, oil, piping and cables, mineral deposits, and missing persons, through the use of divining or dowsing rods. The people were named "water witches" or dowsers. This process has been used as far back as ancient China and was practiced by the early Egyptians. In mediaeval Europe dowsing was quite common until the Holy Inquisition tagged it a form of witchcraft. They burned anyone at the stake for practicing this art, stating that the dowser was communing with the devil. American Marine units reportedly used it to locate booby traps and tunnels in Vietnam.

Great Britain, Holland, and the Soviet Union have officially researched this phenomenon for many years. Soviet experiments indicate that it may be the result of some as-yet-undiscovered form of energy. Experiments have been carried out in Russia where they attached magnets to the dowsers wrists or back. The results have shown the dowser is then incapable of locating buried objects. It has been suggested that a dowser is sensitive to minute magnetic variations in the ground which are produced by the buried substance. The arm muscles will begin to twitch, causing the movement in the rod.

A good dowser can tell you the direction of the water flow, oil, or mineral deposit, its depth, and give a reliable estimate of its volume and pressure. The dowser generally works with a divining rod, which is a forked or "Y" shaped stick cut from a tree like willow, apple, or hazel. You can also use scissors, walking sticks, or clay pipes but the popular alternative to the traditional willow rods are metal "L" rods, which I use. These can be cut and made from wire coat hangers.

Dowsing

Dowsing with Your Hands

There are some who only use their hands, which will quiver and shake like the rod when the right location is found. A friend of my dad's, Rusty O., who was president of his own oil company in Texas, had this talent. When he needed to find another place to drill he would get up at sunrise and go out to the oil fields and walk. When his hand began to shake he knew that the oil was beneath his feet. He did quite well with his own personal dowsing technique.

There are many studies on people who have successfully dowsed from maps, as I can attest to, so the hypothesis is that dowsing is another form of clairvoyance. The dowsing rod is merely the tool which physically indicates, not the means by which the hidden substance is found. You-the human body and mind-are the receiver.

How to Make Your Own Dowsing Rods

There are several different types of dowsing rods on the market, but if you would like to make your own here are a few examples.

Materials Required:
- two metal coat hangers
- a one inch metal tube, one foot long (found at a hardware store)
- metal file

Metal Dowsing Rod Construction:

1. Cut the coat hanger as shown. Smooth off cut edges with a file.

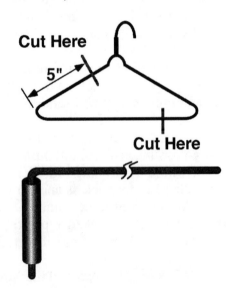

2. Bend coat-hanger wires five inches from one end at a 90 degree angle. Insert these handles into each metal tube.

3. To use, hold rods loosely in each hand parallel to the ground and as stationary as possible. Walk smoothly and steadily to prevent rods from moving. Practice walking so that the rods remain relatively parallel and level.

Traditional Wooden Dowsing Rod Construction:

1. Find a willow, hazel, hawthorn, cherry, or dogwood tree.

2. Cut a Y-shaped branch with 12-to 18-inch arms no thicker than your little finger. Cut branch a few inches down the neck of the Y. Strip off smaller branches.

3. Hold wand in lightly clenched fist with palms facing upward. Neck of wand should be roughly parallel with the ground. Rod will rise or dip sharply when it reacts.

4. Walk slowly. Concentrate on water.

5. Don't worry about whether you are making the wand dip. Just record your results.

Dowsing

Visualization - Getting Everything Out of Your Life

Let's begin with the Meditation Process in the fourth chapter and continue with the following visualization.

You are feeling very relaxed. Gently concentrate on seeing a blank white movie screen in front of your closed eyes. Use your mind like a television screen and put on your screen any picture you want for yourself. Picture yourself floating above the valley in a hot-air balloon still tethered to the ground. (pause) Only by cutting the ropes can you soar to the destination of your dreams.

Now picture yourself standing outside your bosses office. Only by turning the knob and stepping inside can you sell your innovative idea. (pause) Look around you. Are you happy where you are?

Remember everything that you are looking at. (pause) Are you getting everything you want out of your career and life in general? (pause) If not, what's holding you back? (pause) Who's keeping you from cutting those ropes or opening the right door? (pause) Nobody but you!

Remember that the picture you put on your screen must be clear and specific. What you ask for in your life is what you get! (pause) Think first before acting on the thoughts you are going to project. Thoughts are pictures, thought is energy; thoughts are things and you have this power to create pictures of your heart's desire. (pause) Your awareness lies within. (pause) Take this time to look within. (long pause)

Allow yourself to come back into the room and into your body. Feel your body lying on the floor. Close your hands and make a fist. This will circulate all the positive energy through your body.

*Visualize your **White Light** and take in your three deep breaths. Breathe in through the nose and exhaling through your mouth. Breathe in, bringing the **White Light** in through the top of your head. Exhale.*

*Breathe in deeply through your nose and bring the **White Light** down your body.   Exhale*

Breathe in one more time and hold it, hold it, and quickly exhale through your mouth. Then return to regular breathing. (pause) Slowly open your eyes and very slowly sit up. Do not talk. Write down everything that you experienced. If you feel dizzy after any meditation or visualization, close your eyes and take another few deep breaths and tell yourself to come straight back into your body.

Meditation Journal

Day _____   **Time** _____

_____
_____
_____
_____
_____
_____
_____

Dowsing

Exercise 14
Dowsing for Water

Take the phone off the hook, the radio is off, and you will not be disturbed during the exercise.

✔❑ Place a cup of water in the far right corner of the room

✔❑ Hold dowsing rods, one in each hand. Stand at the other end of the room.

✔❑ Take in your three deep breaths and the *White Light* and empty your mind.

✔❑ Look at the rods and concentrate on them as being straight out in front of you.

✔❑ Once they are straight, begin to gently concentrate on water. Keep repeating in your mind "water, water."

✔❑ Begin to walk slowly to the other end of the room, keeping the rods parallel and level.

✔❑ By the time you get near the cup of water, you will feel the rods pulling towards the water.

✔❑ You should end up with the rods pointing directly at the water.

✔❑ Move the water cup around to various parts of the room or outside and watch the rods find the water. This exercise can also be used to find gold, copper, coins, or silver.

Exercise 15
Dowsing for disturbances in the body

✔❑ Hold dowsing rods, one in each hand. Stand at the other end of the room.

✔❑ Take in your three deep breaths and the *White Light* and empty your mind.

✔❑ Look at the rods and concentrate on them as being straight out in front of you.

✔❑ Once they are straight, begin to gently concentrate on the subject. Keep repeating in your mind, "body, body."

✔❑ Begin to slowly walk toward the subject, always keep the rods straight and parallel.

✔❑ When the rods open up, you will know that you have reached the subject's auric field.

✔❑ Stand still and move the rods, up towards the top of the subjects head, always keeping them parallel to the floor. Generally the rods will begin to move in a circular pattern. This will tell you that the subject has a great deal of energy.

Dowsing

✔️❑ If the rod on your right begins to spin around then you will know that this person is very much in his or her conscious mind.

✔️❑ If it begins to spin more on the left side then it is indicating that this person is very creative and spends a great deal of time in the subconscious mind.

✔️❑ Next begin to move down the front of the subject. If the rods move in singularly or together on one place, ask the subject if they have been having problems right there or if they had an operation at that spot. Generally it will be a physical problem or weakness. Continue in this manner down to the feet.

✔️❑ Have the subject turn around and start at the top of the head and go to the feet.

This is a wonderful way of showing, in a physical manner, how electrical disturbances present themselves. I use this frequently when I lecture about medical diagnosing. It is easier to understand when we can see something physical, such as the dowsing rods, showing how the energy in the body is cut off.

Workshop

We had spent a wonderful day learning how to be psychic. Annette Martin's workshop was a hit in my book. We were all standing getting ready to use the dowsing rods. Annette told us we could use these brass rods that had been made especially for her by the famous scientist Marcel Vogel.

"You can use these rods when looking for water, oil, gold, silver, people, whatever you want to find. It is you, not the rods, that is doing the work," Annette told us. "It's as simple as holding the thought in your mind, like water or gold, the rods will turn and point the way for you. Same as the principle of the willow rods bending toward the earth and showing you were to dig for water."

It was my turn and I was excited to try them. We had been doing diagnosing on the body. The dowsing rods had been uncanny in their diagnosis and we were all amazed. As I started to walk forward, dowsing rods in hand, Annette shouted, "Stop! Oh, my God, John, your neck and back are terrible! Your whole back is out of alignment, your right shoulder is in pain and the whole body is wracked with pain. John you have so much pain and had it for so long that you don't even realize that you're in pain. There is like a numbness in the body." She went on, "One of your legs is shorter than the other also and that is throwing the body out of alignment."

I stood there with my mouth open and the others were just staring in awe at Annette's outburst. "John, please you must get to a chiropractor at once, tomorrow! He will adjust you and you will not believe what a different person you will be." Annette immediately ran into her other office and wrote down the name of a chiropractor that she thought could do the trick.

I acknowledged that my back did bother me at times but that I put it out of my mind most of the time and went on with life. My wife has known Annette Martin a long time, so when I returned home and told her of this episode she replied, "I will call the chiropractor tomorrow and get you an appointment."

I don't feel the need to elaborate because everything Annette saw was exactly correct. She was 100% correct. It took six months to get my body back in shape and all I can say is that it is true, I feel like a different person.
　　　　　　　　　　　　　　　　　　　　John Brown

Chapter 15

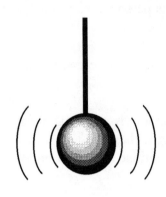

The Guiding Pendulum

What we are and the way we react to the variety of day to day experiences result from reflexes that were developed by our previous experiences. Many of these original experiences, especially the ones that create conflict and frustration, happened when we were young. Consciously they have long since been forgotten, but we continue to react to all types of stimuli in an irrational way, without realizing that our response is due to reflexes that are hidden away in our subconscious mind.

Even the amateur student of psychology knows that if he or she were able to discover the reasons for their reactions to a given stimulus, the student would be able to reduce and eliminate abnormal reactions through understanding, mature insight, and education.

Some people go through psychotherapy and psychoanalysis for weeks, months and, in some cases, years to discover the reasons for their fears and phobias. After exposing the original experience to the light of day, understanding how it was developed and originated, they are then able to reprogram their reflexes to respond in a normal, rational way.

Some years ago a clinical psychologist and author, Leslie M. Le Cron, described a method of retrieving information from the subconscious mind through the autonomic nervous system. The technique has been taught to several thousand physicians. It has been used in many thousands of cases to great advantage, even by a number of psychiatrists. You can learn this technique very easily. And you can discover by communicating directly with the subconscious mind, why you react as you do, what caused the original reflex, and why the experience created your present-day anxieties.

The technique is called the Pendulum Method. I will describe what you must do and how you can expect to get a response. But first, I want to explain that for hundreds of years the pendulum has been used as an attempt to foretell the future. Our use of it is merely a device to gain information from the subconscious mind. It is by far the easiest and quickest way to learn the causes of emotional disturbances and other conditions.

Pendulum Method

In using the pendulum you should hold the thread or chain between the thumb and forefinger, with your elbow resting on the arm of your chair on a desk, or perhaps on your knee. The weight then dangles freely.

Four basic directions of movement of the pendulum are possible. The movement can be in a clockwise circle, counter-clockwise circle, back and forth across in front of you, or in and out away from you. The inner (subconscious) can be asked to make its own selection of movements.

One motion is to signify yes. A second means no. A third should mean I don't know. The fourth means I do not want to answer the question.

You may specify the meaning of each movement, but it is better to let the subconscious make its own selections. This seems to bring better cooperation on its part. It also shows you that the subconscious does not think and reason.

Pendulum

Exercise 16
Pendulum

✔❑ Hold the pendulum. Voluntarily move it in each of the four directions, then hold it motionless and ask which is to mean yes. In doing this no words are usually necessary. You merely think the request.

✔❑ The subconscious is asked to select any of the four motions which is then to represent an affirmative reply. You might word your request this way :

"My subconscious is to select one of these four motions of this pendulum to mean yes in answer to the question." The pendulum will work better if you watch it.

✔❑ Usually it will start to move within a few seconds, but sometimes it may take a moment or so to "warm up the motor." If it does not start to swing very quickly, think the word yes to yourself several times. Be sure you do not move the pendulum voluntarily. Try to hold it still, but you will find it will move of its own accord. If you still find there is no movement, have someone else ask the questions to establish the four movements for reply.

✔❑ When your affirmative response has been set up, ask for selection of another motion to mean no, then for one of the two remaining ones to mean I don't know. The fourth will then represent not wanting to answer.

✔❑ You will find this very interesting. Many people exclaim in surprise as the pendulum swings in answering. Movements may be somewhat slight, but usually the arc of the swing is long and very definite.

There is nothing magical or spooky in this. It merely shows to the most skeptical that the subconscious mind does think, and also that it is able to control muscular movements. The subconscious continually controls such movements. As you read this it is controlling your breathing muscles. When you walk you do not think of all the movements involved and the necessary coordination, although you had to learn these as a child.

After you had practiced a bit and fallen many times, you set up a conditioned reflex and your subconscious took over control of the muscles involved. Your movements in walking then became involuntary. The same is true in learning to type. Your typing would be very slow if you had to think consciously of how to strike each key.

Have fun and answer your innermost questions.

Chapter 16

Automatic Writing

Automatic writing, as the name suggests, involves the spontaneous writing of coherent messages, usually in a different handwriting and often while the subject is talking about something entirely different or is in an altered state of consciousness.

The chief characteristic of automatic writing as a phenomenon is the subject's conviction that he or she is not in control of their hand. Reportedly, the writing goes on without the subject's intervention; in fact, conscious efforts to interfere with it are often overridden and, at best, result in a distortion in the flow of the handwriting.

The subconscious mind can control the muscles of your hand and write intelligibly without you being consciously aware of what is being written. Sometimes it writes backward or with the other hand while the first hand is writing consciously.

Differences in the choice of words and in the order in which they are put together are also commonly reported. There is almost universal agreement among successful practitioners that the hand moves across the page in a different way than normal, and all reports indicate that automatic writing feels different from normal writing. There are even reports that when this phenomenon is applied to the typewriter or computer, the characteristic way in which the typist hits the keys is changed.

In automatic writing the subject sits in a chair and simply moves a pencil in circles until it begins to write coherent answers to questions, seemingly of its own volition. This is sometimes reported to be accompanied by hearing what is being written before it is actually spelled out. However, what is heard is usually spoken in a voice completely unlike the voice the subject usually hears inside his or her head.

A number of novels have allegedly been written in this fashion, and both art and music have been produced automatically, most notably a number of Bach fugues produced by a housewife with no knowledge of classical music.

An ideal way of gaining information from the subconscious is through automatic writing. Our subconscious knows what is causing emotional and psychosomatic illnesses. Questions may be asked and replies written out. At times the subconscious may volunteer information.

In automatic writing, words generally run together, and the letters may be malformed and difficult to read. I know my first attempts at automatic writing were pages upon pages of just lines and then finally words began to appear that all ran together. The writing may be backwards, upside down, mirror images, or condensed, such as "4 u" instead of "for you."

Practice makes perfect, so let's begin.

Automatic Writing

> ## Exercise 17
> ## Practicing automatic writing

Make sure the phone is off the hook and the radio is turned off. Find a quiet place to practice.

✔❑ Sit in a comfortable chair without arms; preferably use a hard writing surface across the knees. A desk top may be used but can restrict the movement of the arm.

✔❑ Use a soft pencil or thick ball-point pen. I prefer a pencil, for the energy seems to be more easily directed through the lead in the pencil. Hold it vertically between the thumb and fore finger. Start at the top left of the page with the point resting on the paper.

✔❑ Now it is time to tell your subconscious mind that you would like to have it control your hand. Take in your three deep breaths, with the *White Light* of course, and write your name at the top of the page.

✔❑ Then make a few circles to loosen up your hand and arm and return the pencil or pen to the upper left- hand corner.

✔❑ Make no voluntary movement. The hand may not move for several minutes. When it does begin to move of its own accord, it may make only lines or geometric figures, as though warming up.

✔❑ Watch your hand closely and keep thinking that it is going to begin to move. Then relax your mind, feel it in a void space. You may begin to feel a tingling sensation in the muscles of your arm, or that the arm is no longer a part of you. If you begin to write try not to anticipate the words that come out.

✔❑ The handwriting will not be your usual writing. Movements may be jerky; they may move slowly or race across the page.

✔❑ You may close your eyes to keep from anticipating or focusing on what is being written.

✔❑ If the hand does not move for 20 minutes, stop and try a second time later.

Do not be discouraged. Probably no more than one out of five people can write automatically without considerable effort and practice. However your chances are quite high that you will be able to so, in due time.

Automatic Writing

Homework

1. Set a time and day in the next week, when you will practice using the **Pendulum.** Just keep track of your experiences.

QUESTION	Yes	No
1. _____	✔❑	✔❑
2. _____	✔❑	✔❑
3. _____	✔❑	✔❑

2. Set a time and day in the next week, when you will practice using **Automatic Writing.** Just keep track of your experiences.

QUESTIONS:

1. _____
2. _____
3. _____
4. _____
5. _____

ANSWERS:

1. _____
2. _____
3. _____
4. _____
5. _____

Chapter 17

Imagery - Visualization and Your Goals

In 1975, I became actively involved teaching classes in psychic development and meditation for the Center for Attitudinal Healing, headed by the well-known psychiatrist, author, and lecturer, Dr. Gerald Jampolsky. We used biofeedback machines in conjunction with visualization techniques for many of the cancer patients who were suffering from severe headaches due to their chemotherapy and other drugs.

Connectors from the biofeedback machines were wrapped around the fore finger on the right and left hands, the patients were asked to close their eyes, visualize their hands, and feel the hands getting warmer and warmer. Upon opening their eyes they could see for themselves that the dials had moved up, indicating their hands were becoming warmer. After awhile they could do this on their own and soon began to control the upcoming headache.

At the Diamond Headache Clinic in Chicago, migraine patients use imagery to abort headaches by vividly picturing their hands over a hot fire or radiator. "Raising hand temperature with the mind is very effective," says Seymour Diamond, M. D., director of the clinic. "Why or how, no one knows for sure."

One of the theories is that it redirects blood flow, diverting blood away from the head to the extremities. Another is that it causes a "neural reflex" in nerves that control the blood vessels in the head. What is most interesting is that when the patients put their hands in hot water, the headaches were not affected. When the patient was coached to picture the heat generated by their mind, bingo, that did the trick.

See What It Is You Want, Then Do It

Using imaging for success has been popular for years with high-powered business executives, people committed to securing every possible advantage for success, and with Olympic athletes. Numerous studies have proven that it works. What people are able to see they're more likely to be able to do.

We are going to practice this technique and you will soon experience for yourselves the amazing feats that your mind can accomplish.

I firmly believe that all that's needed is to create an image of the desired outcome exactly how you want it to be. That holds true for any situation or disease because everyone wants to become a healthy and functioning human being.

I had spent a year working at KGU Talk Radio in Honolulu, Hawaii. Being a morning radio hostess, up at three in the morning, to be ready to talk and be intelligent for three hours and a daily hour psychic show had put a toll on my health. While flying back from Hawaii to California in 1982, this poem came to me.

The Windows of My Mind

Oh, how I look through
the windows of my mind.
With great expectations
to happen in time.

It does not always appear
as I see it in my mind.
Perhaps, I am trying so hard
that the creation blows it out of my mind.

I love the pictures that lie there
all nestled and ready to develop.
What if I leave them alone and
allow them their time to be born.

My mind is full of ideas, perhaps if I trust
and believe, I know that it will appear.

O' beauteous white light, reflect and help me to see
Into the windows of me.

> Remember, you always get
> what you want, which may not
> be what you're asking for.

Visualization is a very powerful tool, which, when used indiscriminately, can actually be destructive to your goals.

Begin With A Choice

* **Choice has power:**
    When you make a choice, you focus great human energy and resources that normally go untapped.

* **How to make a choice:**
    Ask the right question. Example: "What is it I really want?"

At any time, regardless of the circumstances, you can always ask and answer this question. Do not limit yourself based on what you think is possible.

This takes practice, for in childhood we are taught to censor our dreams and visions down to realistic proportions. More than half of what we learn growing up is what we "can't" have and what we "shouldn't" do. ("Don't talk to strangers." "Don't run across the street." "Don't play with matches.")

Imagery - Visualization

These phrases leave us with a general impression of limitation long after we know how to cross the street safely, light a match and talk to people we have just met.

Remember to always identify all of what you want, including the circumstances and consequences of getting what you want..

Example: A young woman said she wanted to be more assertive. When asked if she had any doubts that she wanted more assertiveness in her personality, she thought for a moment and said, "Yes, if I were more assertive, I'm afraid that people wouldn't like me."

As you can see the young woman wanted two things: to be assertive and to be liked be others.

We need to see the whole picture: what you want, the circumstances surrounding what you want, and the long-term consequences you desire. Once you have identified what you want, asked this test question:

"If I could have it, would I take it?" If the answer is "yes," you really do want it. If the answer is "no," you probably do not really want it. If your answer to the question is "yes," now is the time to formally choose what you want. Repeat the words, "I chose (what you want)".

As you say the words, get a sense of choosing inwardly as well.

Goals

* Main Choice: This is a choice about major results. One which you see having general importance in your life. This includes committing yourself to do whatever it takes to live in accordance with that choice.

* Secondary Choice: Example: You have chosen to have a job (main choice), secondary choices may include fulfilling the requirements of the position (being at work on time).

Write a practice goal for each week. If it will be a major upset if you do not achieve this goal, choose another goal. Do not choose a goal that is an issue for you. Example: quitting smoking for the last ten years and have been unsuccessful, don't make it your practice goal to become a non-smoker. Start out with small goals and work up to the big things.

If your goal is too vague, too general, or not clearly defined, the subconscious has a difficult time understanding what you want. Your practice goal may be material or non-material.

Form your practice goal in the present, as if it were already accomplished - the full and complete result you want. If you see your goal occurring in the future, the subconscious will be less likely to assist you in creating what you want now, because, to the subconscious, the future is always in the future. Keep your goal to yourself, talking about it dissipates energy and focus.

Make sure your goal is a result that you want, not a process toward some result.

Take five minutes a day and visualize this goal. See it occurring on your blank screen, the windows of your mind. Write a concise description of your goal. Include your feelings as well. Draw a picture if you like.

Imagery - Visualization

1st week - goal

_____

2nd week - goal

_____

3rd week - goal

_____

4th week - goal

_____

106

Imagery - Visualization

Visualization - Raising the Body Temperature

Let's begin with the Meditation Process in Chapter 4, then continue with the following.

You are feeling very relaxed. I want you look at your large, white movie screen. The entire screen is blank. Imagine yourself on the white screen. You are lying on the floor, very comfortable and relaxed. Focus on your feet, see your feet. Feel a wonderful warm wind enter your toes and slowly move to the rest of your feet. Your feet are feeling warmer and warmer, toasty warm.

Take in a deep breath and exhale your warm breath into your feet. Good. With all that nice heat that you have built in your feet begin to move it up your calves. See your calf muscles getting warmer and warmer, moving up to your knees and thighs. In your mind's eye see both of your legs and feet glowing with the wonderful heat that you have manufactured.

Look at your legs. Take in a deep breath and exhale your warm breath into your legs. Good. Feel and see the heat rising up into the trunk of your body. First the abdomen. The heat could look like flames from a fire or heat billowing out of a pot belly stove. However you wish to picture the heat is perfect. See your body on the screen and see the heat rising through your abdomen.

Move around to your hips and direct the flames or billowing heat to your hips. See your body and the heat going around to your hips. Allow this heat to travel up your spine. Feel your back beginning to relax, deeper and deeper as the heat pervades every crevice.
(Pause)

*Close your hands and make a fist. Breathe in deeply through your nose and visualize the **White Light** coming down in through the top of your head. Exhale through your mouth. Breathe in again deeply through your nose, exhale through your mouth . One last time, breathe in deeply and hold it, hold it, and exhale quickly through your mouth. You are feeling calm and peaceful. **Write down everything that you experienced during the meditation and visualization.***

Meditation Journal

Day _____ **Time** _____

_____
_____
_____
_____
_____
_____
_____
_____
_____
_____
_____
_____
_____

Chapter 18

Symbols

Dr. Karl Zener invented a deck of special cards for telepathy research. These cards have been used extensively in ESP experiments. Each white Zener card bears one of five basic symbols colored black: a star, cross, circle, square, and three wavy lines. There are 25 cards in the deck, so each symbol is represented five times.

Before we experiment with this exercise we are going to do our Meditation:

Lowering the Body Temperature

Let's begin with the Meditation Process in Chapter 4, then continue with the following.

On your white movie screen, see yourself sitting on a hot, dry beach in Florida. (pause) The wind is warm and humid, the ocean water is warm, and you have run out of water to drink.

The sand is sticking to your perspiring body and you are feeling hotter by the minute. Your hands feel a bit swollen and your feet are burning up. (pause)

Focus on the top of your head. (pause)   Visualize someone coming over with a bucket of cool water. They are going to pour this cool water down the back of your head, which will flow down your neck onto your shoulders. (pause)

Ah, it's so cooling and refreshing. Now, feel and see this cool water being poured onto your chest and flowing down your arms and hands. (pause) Your hands are so much better, they're feeling cool and not swollen from the heat. (pause)

The cool water is running down your abdomen and down to your legs. Another bucket is poured down the front of you, this time your legs are beginning to feel cool and your hot and dry body is relaxing. (pause)

More water is poured down your shoulders and onto your back and hips. (pause) You're feeling so much better and cooler. (pause)

Symbols

The bucket has been filled again with cool water and you are going to stick your two feet inside the bucket. (pause) Ah, now you are really feeling cool. It's delightful. The stickiness on your skin is gone and you are feeling so comfortable. (pause)

Sit and enjoy the coolness in your body. (long pause)

Now, see yourself sitting in the same place. (pause) Your body is feeling normal and comfortable. (pause)

Close your hands and make a fist.

*Breathe in deeply through your nose and visualize the **White Light** coming down in through the top of your head. Exhale through your mouth.*

Breathe in again deeply through your nose, exhale through your mouth .

One last time, breathe in deeply and hold it, hold it, and exhale quickly through your mouth. You are feeling calm and peaceful.

Write down everything that you experienced during the meditation and visualization.

Meditation Journal

Day _____ **Time** _____

_____
_____
_____
_____
_____
_____
_____
_____
_____
_____
_____
_____
_____
_____
_____
_____
_____
_____

Symbols

Exercise 18
Zener cards
This requires a partner

✔❑ Sit apart from your partner, who should not be able to see the card faces and who should be supplied with a pad to record guesses. Shuffle the cards well and place them face downwards in front of you.

✔❑ Sender when the receiver is ready pick up the first card and look at it, and send the symbol telepathically to the receiver. Once the receiver has recorded a guess, place that card face down on the table and start another pile, then take an other card and repeat the process. Continue until you finish the entire deck.

✔❑ Call out the card symbols in the order they appeared and have the receiver or receivers check them off the list.

Chance would score: **5 correct**
A score of: **7 correct - is odds of 20 to 1**
This score and above are listed as significant and demonstrative of extra-sensory perception.
A score of: **8 correct - odds of 250 to 1**

If you do not have a set of Zener cards then please use the following exercise.

Exercise 19
Sending a symbol
This requires a partner

✔❑ **You will need blank white paper and colored crayons or colored pencils.**

✔❑ Sit on the floor or in chairs, with your backs to each other. Decide which person will be the Sender of the symbol and which person will be the Receiver. Enter your names in the following score sheet.

✔❑ Each take a blank piece of paper.

✔❑ There is to be no talking during this exercise.

✔❑ Put a time clock out for yourselves and **set it for 10 minutes.**

✔❑ Do the following Sender / Receiver exercise once.

✔❑ Mark down on the following page your score and discuss for a few moments what you experienced with your partner.

✔❑ Switch Sender and Receiver.

✔❑ Repeat the process over again. Put down your score and discuss your progress.

Symbols

✔❏ **Sender** Choose a crayon without your partner knowing what color you are going to use. Take your paper, crayon, or colored pencil, choose one of the below symbols, and draw it. It can be the star, heart, cross, circle, arrow, triangle, or rectangle shape. But only choose one!

Make it simple! Only one shape. Make the shape large enough to cover the entire sheet of paper. After you draw it initially, then keep going over the drawing with your crayon. Concentrate only on the shape you have drawn, nothing else.

✔❏ **Receiver** Close your eyes and begin your breathing. Breath in through your nose and bring in the *White Light*. Exhale through your mouth. Do this three times.

Bring up your blank, white movie screen. Take a few more breaths if you need to and allow the symbol and color to come over to you on your screen. Don't try to see the symbol or the color. Just allow it to come to you. Be gentle with yourself, be kind to yourself. If you try to make it happen, it will not work.

When we try or force ourselves to do anything we are then creating a resistance. This is applicable to everything in life. So pay attention to what it is you are doing. As soon as you begin to get an impression, draw on the paper what you feel, hear, sense, know, or see the sender is drawing. Allow the shape and the color to come gently over to you. Write down the name of the color on your blank piece of paper.

Symbol & Color Score Sheet

Date	Sender	Receiver	Sender	Receiver
Names				
Symbol				
Color				
Names				
Symbol				
Color				
Names				
Symbol				
Color				

Symbols

Homework

Symbol & Color Score Sheet

Date	Sender	Receiver	Sender	Receiver
Names				
Symbol				
Color				
Names				
Symbol				
Color				
Names				
Symbol				
Color				

Chapter 19

Clairvoyance - Remote Viewing

Clairvoyance is long- range telepathy and is treated as a separate form of ESP because the explanations of extended sensation do not apply. Clairvoyance is the direct perception of some fact not already present in any human mind - e.g., the symbol on a card which nobody has yet looked at. Clairvoyance usually takes place over distances of hundreds or thousands of miles.

Since the 1930's efforts have been made to overcome these difficulties by controlled experiments to test the presence of ESP. The pioneer was the famous Dr. J. B. Rhine of Duke University, North Carolina. Briefly, the idea is to provide, say, a pack of 25 cards, each bearing one of five symbols, so that there are five cards of each symbol. Thus the chance of a person correctly guessing the symbol appearing on a particular card is one in five, or 20 percent. If a person consistently guesses correctly a much larger percentage some force other than chance must be assumed to be operative. By eliminating every possible know factor one may reach the conclusion that the operative factor is an unknown faculty of the mind. This, for want of a better name, we call the psi faculty or ESP.

The best evidence for the existence of clairvoyance are the experiments conducted at Stanford Research Institute by Harold Puthoff and Russell Targ, described in their book Mind-Reach. They conducted a series of double-blind experiments, that is, experiments in which neither experimenter nor subject know the necessary information for successful completion of the experiment - e.g., the symbol on a card which nobody has yet looked at. This prevents the experimenter from inadvertently giving hints to the correct answers. Telepathy and clairvoyance are both forms of ESP.

An explosive prediction

Evidence for ESP falls into two categories: spontaneous and experimental. Here is a letter about a well-known event I predicted on May 22, 1980:

Dear Diane Raymond:

It was great talking with you yesterday. As I stated in our conversation regarding the prediction I made on May 11, 1980. It was like a bolt out of the sky, when I relayed to my friend Gary, "Be careful next week while driving up the Oregon coast line. I have a terrible feeling that there is going to be a volcanic explosion and an earthquake or two. I feel very nervous about you driving along the coast." **As we all know Mt. St. Helen's erupted on the 18th of May without warning and created two earthquakes along the coastline.**

I am not a doomsday psychic ; however, I feel prompted to forward the following prediction to you for the record and will announce it on my radio show next week.

Clairvoyance

Today is May 22, 1980 and I see Mt. St. Helens will erupt again within the week. The ashes from Mt. St. Helens will cover all of the U. S. The ash has radioactive particles that will bring about a great deal of deaths to animal, plant life and affect human life. I also see Mt. Hood becoming active and shaking and many earthquakes in the area.

Sincerely,   Annette Martin

Published reports: **May 24, 1980 San Francisco Chronicle**
Second eruption of Mt. St. Helens with ash cloud that is spreading radioactive gas across U.S.

"Annette Martin Was the Only Published Psychic to Predict Mt. St. Helens Erupting"
       Headline Los Altos Town Crier and Peninsula Times Tribune.

Second prediction and published report:

June 11, 1980 on my Telepsychic Radio Show I announced that another eruption of Mt. St. Helens would occur that week between 6/12 & 6/16/80.

June 13, 1980 San Jose News Volcano explodes for the third time. Mt. St. Helens erupted during the night.

Third prediction and published report:

April 5, 1981, predicted on my radio show: "I see Mt. St. Helens blowing again between April 10, 1981 & April 13, 1981.

San Jose News, Mt. St. Helens erupted again on April 10, 1981

Ideal Conditions

We are going to conduct our own long-range telepathy experiments using this same process, but before we begin we need to look at the ideal experimental conditions used with successful experiments:

- an emotionally aroused sender
- a sleeping receiver or one producing a steady alpha rhythm, such as when meditating
- the creation of a strong mental image by the sender
- a strong visualization of the receiver by the sender
- a strong intention to send the message
- a belief that such communication is possible

Clairvoyance

Remote Viewing

The Encyclopedia of Parapsychology and Psychical Research (1991)
"Remote Viewing: A protocol to test for extrasensory perception."

On December 8, 1971, the American Society for Psychical Research (ASPR) in New York in association with Dr. G. Schmeidler, Dr. K. Osis, Dr. J. Mitchell, and the gifted artist and pioneer in the field of psychic research, Ingo Swan, coined the term "remote viewing." It was called such to identify a particular kind of experiment-not particularly a kind of psychic or psi ability.

Remote viewing received international merit after 1974 at Stanford Research Institute (SRI) under the auspices of Dr. H. E.. Puthoff and Mr. Russell Targ. Experiments have what in science are called "protocols or "steps" that govern how the experiment is executed. The last step which involves determining whether the experiment worked or not, or how well it worked, is called "feed back."

Without feedback in some form, it cannot be known if the experiment worked. Positive feedback tells us that there is a possible utilitarian value; negative feedback, or the absence of it, does not.

Different kinds of experiments need to be distinguished from one another and in the case of the term remote viewing there can be no doubt at all that it originally referred to an experimental model (never to a novel ESP ability) and there exists an enormous archive of paperwork on the subject.

Visualization - Good Qualities & Weaknesses

Let's begin with the Meditation Process in the fourth chapter and continue with the following visualization.

You are feeling very relaxed. Gently concentrate on seeing a blank white movie screen in front of your closed eyes. See a large black marker in your hands and draw on your movie screen all of your good endearing qualities. (pause) Good.

Now look at your words and read them back to yourself in your mind.

Remember everything that you are looking at. (pause) Do you like all those qualities? (pause)
Do you want to add more to the list? Go ahead and add more, if you like. (pause)
Acknowledge these good qualities about yourself. Tell yourself that these are some of the most wonderful things you like about yourself. (pause)

Now, take your large black marker and scroll down your screen, so that it is blank once more. That's it, now write down on the screen some of your weaknesses. (pause) Be truthful with yourself, really examine your vulnerabilities.

Remember everything that you are looking at.   (pause)

How are you learning to deal with your weaknesses? (pause) Do you brush them under the rug or do you address them from time to time? (pause)

You have examined your good qualities and your weaknesses, now see how you can use them both to

Clairvoyance

make your life better and make you a stronger person. (long pause)

Allow yourself to come back into the room and into your body. Feel your body lying on the floor.

Close your hands and make a fist. This will circulate all the positive energy through your body.

*Visualize your **White Light** and take in your three deep breaths. Remembering to breathe in through the nose and exhaling through your mouth.*

Let's begin:

*Breathe in, bringing the **White Light** in through the top of your head.   Exhale.*

*Breathe in deeply through your nose and bring the **White Light** down your body.   Exhale*

Breathe in one more time and hold it, hold it and quickly exhale through your mouth. Then return to regular breathing. (pause) Slowly open your eyes and very slowly sit up. Do not talk. Write down everything that you experienced. If you feel dizzy after any meditation or visualization close your eyes and take another few deep breaths and tell yourself to come straight back into your body.

Meditation Journal

Day _____   **Time** _____

_____
_____
_____
_____
_____
_____
_____
_____
_____
_____
_____
_____
_____
_____
_____
_____
_____
_____
_____
_____

Clairvoyance

Exercise 20
Remote viewing
This requires a partner

Use an object that is easy to recognize. If you use a complicated object at first, you will probably experience confusion of bits and pieces of information. As an example, start with a simple gold necklace or a string of pearls rather than a necklace that has a complicated design.

✔❑　You will need blank white paper and a pen or pencil.

✔❑　**Sender** Go into another room and place one object on a table. If another room is not available, the object can be placed in a closed box or simply behind a barrier that you can't see through.

✔❑　**Sender** Let **receiver** know you are ready by voice contact only.

✔❑　**Receiver** Date and put the time you begin on the piece of paper in the upper right hand corner. Take in your three deep breaths and the *White Light* and bring up your blank white movie screen. Write down all the images that flash across your mind, do not discount anything. If you do not see things then write out the feelings you have, or what it reminds you of. Be sure to put everything down on the paper, drawing is very important. Your own sixth sense will produce the pictures for you, frequently without the aid or understanding of consciousness. Many people try to develop their sixth sense by using only the conscious mental awareness.

By not making a picture drawing, you will not have a chance to see how your sixth sense is processing.

✔❑　Do this exercise for only 10 minutes.

✔❑　**Receiver** Put your pencil or pen down, close your hands and take in your three deep breaths and *White Light*. Then ask for immediate feedback from the sender.

✔❑　Compare your drawing and notes with the sender. After a few tries, you will feel like you are getting the hang of it and you will begin to note the specifics of the information you are receiving.

I have found there are four major types of associations when we receive incoming messages in our sixth sense. They have not emerged as the exact drawing but have activated our emotions, taste, hearing, smell, etc.

1. Something that the object (or place) reminds you of
2. A picture of something very similar to the object
3. Things associated with the object, or that might be expected to be associated with it
4. Emotions that are associated

✔❑　**Sender** and **receiver** take three turns each and mark on following score sheet.

Clairvoyance

Remote Viewing Results

Day _____ **Time** _____

Sender:

_____
_____
_____
_____
_____
_____
_____
_____
_____
_____

Receiver:

_____
_____
_____
_____
_____
_____
_____
_____
_____
_____

Clairvoyance

> ## Exercise 21
> # Long distance remote viewing
> This requires three people

✔❑ **Destination selector-Receiver-Sender.** Directions to five sites, five envelopes, large manila envelope, paper for sketching, two tape recorders

✔❑   Two days before the exercise in remote-viewing, have the **destination selector** choose five locations within a 20 minute drive of where the experiment is to take place. Write out specific directions on how to get there by car. **Destination selector** must seal each set of directions in a separate business- size envelope and seal all five of these envelopes in a large manila envelope. These are to be held by the recorder until the experiment begins.

✔❑   On the day of the exercise have the **sender, receiver, and destination selector** meet together to synchronize watches. Destination selector will give the sender the envelopes containing the directions and begin timing. The remote-viewing should take place exactly 45 minutes later. The sender should get in the car, with the tape recorder and drive at least a mile from the place where the class or experiment is being conducted before opening one, and only one, of the sets of directions. The other four business envelopes need to be put back into the manila envelope unopened.

✔❑   **Sender** Follow instructions to the target location. When sender arrives, which should be 45 minutes after the experiment began, begin to walk around the target area. Set your timer for 20 minutes and begin to talk into the tape recorder about what you are seeing, feeling, touching, and experiencing in the surroundings at the target site. Focus on where you are, do not think of other things. Don't try to send what you are experiencing, just observe and touch them. At the end of the 20 minutes return to your car and return to original destination.

✔❑   **Receiver** Do meditation without visualization, while **sender** is traveling. At a designated time, you can set a timer to help remember, **receiver** needs to turn on the tape recorder and have paper and pencil ready. Stay very relaxed and just watch your blank movie screen for scenes or objects. Talk out loud into your tape recorder, about whatever images flash into your mind. Don't leave anything out because you think it's not noteworthy. That could be the very thing that is the subject of the target area. Draw pictures of what you are seeing, feeling, knowing, smelling. Describe everything. Even if the pictures or feelings seem silly say them out loud and draw them on your paper. We all perceive things differently so it is important to verbalize and draw so you will be able to correlate what is being sent.

✔❑ **Sender** Return to original destination.

✔❑   **Receiver** Play the tape and show pictures to **sender**. Your **destination selector** can be a judge as to how accurate you were.

This exercise can also be done long distance via tape recording. Make copies for each other and mail to each other to see how accurate you were. It can be lots of fun, perhaps with a pen pal.

Clairvoyance

Homework

Choose a partner to work with. Ask your partner to use an object that is easy to recognize. If you use a complicated object at first, you will probably experience a confusion of bits and pieces of information. As an example, start with a simple gold necklace or a string of pearls rather than a necklace that has a complicated design. Remember to make it simple and you will have much more success. Set a time and day next week when you will practice your remote viewing. You can do this as often as you wish. Just keep track of your experiences.

Write down in your workbook if you are to be the sender or the receiver and always record your observations.

Object _____**Receiver** _____**Date** _____**Time**_____

_____

_____

_____

_____

_____

Object _____**Receiver** _____**Date** _____**Time**_____

_____

_____

_____

_____

_____

_____

Object _____**Receiver** _____**Date** _____**Time**_____

_____

_____

_____

_____

_____

Object _____**Receiver** _____**Date** _____**Time**_____

Chapter 20

_____

_____

_____

_____

_____

Clairaudience
and
Becoming Your Animal

Clairaudience is the paranormal hearing of sounds like music, thunder, voices, gun-fire, etc. which have no physical source and which are often not heard by others.

Clairaudience has been reported throughout history, but it is rarely admitted to because it has come to be regarded as an indication of incipient insanity.

Schizophrenics and other mentally deranged people claim that the devil, God, spirits, or a deceased person speaks to them. We have seen many cases of homicide when the accused declares that "the voices made me do it." This does not mean that all those who hear voices, occasionally or frequently, are mentally ill.

We need to understand how our brains function auditorily. The sound we ordinarily hear when someone speaks or a dog barks is not "out there" in the sense that it is just piped into our brains via our ears. These sounds do not have an objective reality; rather, we create them in the hearing centers of our brains from the auditory impulses that are produced in the inner ear by vibrations in the air, the sound waves. Does a dog whistle make a sound when it is blown? To you it doesn't, but to the dog-which is sensitive to sound waves of a much higher frequency-it does.

Hearing is our second most developed sense and I feel in many ways is as remarkable as our sight. When we hear a sound that has no outside source, it can only mean that the hearing centers of the brain have been activated, either by a mental malfunction or by a paranormal stimulus. The latter results in clairaudience.

We all have chatter going on inside of our heads. This is what writers call "internal monologue," though often there is more than one voice in conversation. If you hear voices and want to turn them off, use the same technique that you use every day when you want to listen to just one person in a crowded room or when you want to study undisturbed by street noises, television or conversations. Focus your attention on something else that is more interesting to you. If you hadn't noticed, everything thrives on attention; by withdrawing your attention and focusing somewhere else, you take away the energy that keeps unwanted inner voices active. It doesn't matter whether this is a soul that has departed the earth or someone in the body, when you stop paying attention eventually they will stop talking to you.

Clairaudience Examples

On Sept. 14, 1979, my advanced Psychic Development class settled on the floor. I closed my eyes, for half a second and then they flew open. Leaning over to my secretary, I whispered, "Kay, quick, put on the tape recorder, someone is trying to come through."

Kay, responded immediately and I began to speak in a deep, clear masculine voice, "Please, listen carefully to what I have to say. It is most important."

Clairaudience

Everyone was silent, paying close attention, as the voice presented this poem, with barely a breath between phrases.

THE CHILD

Be not just a child when you are children, but be the child
when you are the adult as well. Look to the child for your
feelings, as well as look to the adult for your feelings.

Look to the male energy and look to the female energy. Expose
them both for what they are, for that is truly what you are -
the intermingling of the two as the branches intertwine together.
So this is you!

Look at these two aspects and do not be ashamed of either for
they do not come out as a forked tongue, but as one tongue.

Be thou still and quiet, my children, for you shall see the
light and the light is within you and without you. To be still
and know is the answer. The quietness is within, the joy is
without — synonymous within each other.

Feel the calmness and the joy, for then doth the light appear
within the eyes with which you see and thru the eyes, like the
mirror that is reflected to thee.

I speak to you of the morrow for as each second slips by
tis thus that you are in the morrow.

Go quietly yet swiftly; Go calmly but joyfully.

The child must never die without his delight in himself. The
movement within the child and the adult creates growth. Growth,
my children is like watching the waves upon the sea; as they gather
their strength they roll into the shore and they move from the shore
and gather in the water and the energy and come pounding back
again to repeat the process over and over again.

You are the sea! You are that movement!
Experience that movement!

We have gathered you together and taken you by the hand
and now you must move within the movement. It will be
easy. But as you should slip, remember the child, and this will
strike a familiar chord of remembrance.

You will play a symphony upon the Earth. Each of you - the cast
of a thousand — each playing his or her own symphony.
Remember the time is always now.

I bid you farewell until we meet again.

Omar Kyan

Clairaudience

Another example

A young man had started a new job at a grocery store 800 hundred miles away from his home. One day while waiting on a customer he suddenly heard his mother call out to him and without thinking he turned and replied, "Yes, mother?" He was both surprised and embarrassed to discover that his mother was not there and could only apologetically explain to the customer that he had seemingly heard his mother speak to him.

The young man wrote to his mother and described what had happened. She wrote back, "That's the day I was working in the basement and needed a hand with carrying a box upstairs and called out to you to help." She had apparently forgotten he wasn't at home anymore and called him, fully expecting him to be there. Then she realized he was living in an other town and felt funny about it.

This incident may have been caused by the mother's thoughts telepathically stimulating her son's hearing centers, thereby producing the illusion that she had called him from nearby.

Last year my eldest son, Craig, was ill with a virus. He went to bed, fell asleep, and suddenly heard my voice calling him. Craig and his family live a good 60 miles away. Craig called me on the phone about an hour later and asked if I had been thinking about him. I answered, "I was worried about your health and have been sending my healing White goop to you. I also called your name, several times, in my mind."

Clairaudiently heard voices may belong to those who are living or who are dead, or they may apparently originate from a spiritual entity. The voice may call out the person's name, or it may offer advice, warn of danger, or even predict the future. In the introduction I spoke about the baritone voice that told me to "pick up that stick," that literally saved my life. That was indeed a clairaudient experience.

In numerous books it's been written that the Greek philosopher Socrates was frequently counseled by a voice he called his daimon or deity, which helped him to make the right decisions and live correctly.

Joan of Arc, the maid of Orleans, France, was another historical personage who received instructions and guidance from disembodied voices. She began to hear these voices at the age of 16 years old. These voices continually encouraged her to take up arms against the English invaders of France.

In North American Indian culture, which implicitly believes in a spirit world, every young boy and girl was expected to acquire a spirit guide who would remain with them throughout life and give them a certain power. The ones who had the most talent in this area became the medicine men and women. The guardian spirit quest usually took place between the ages of 10 and 14. The child was instructed: "It is time for you to fast and seek out your spirit guide. It will give you your special power and be your guide throughout your life. You will call upon it whenever you need it."

Clairaudient experiences will often happen in times of danger. The voice will suggest what you are to do, which in my case has saved my life numerous times.

Visualization - Understanding Your Hearing

Let's begin with the Meditation Process in Chapter 4 then continue with the following.

On your blank white movie screen, focus in on the top of your head. (pause) Now, look around the

Clairaudience

different parts of your head. (pause)

Look at your ears and the level of them. (pause) Become aware of the area about one or two inches above your ears. (pause) Notice how this area has a higher sensitivity. (pause) In your mind see a large speaker getting ready to amplify sounds to your ears. (pause)

On your screen take yourself to a place where you can hear many people talking. Your inner speaker is turned up and you can hear many conversations going on. (pause) Find a bench, chair, or something to sit on and listen to the different conversations. (pause)

Now, listen to the background noise or conversations. (long pause) Become aware that your sense of sound is outside of you, in the short distance.

Now we are going to focus on talking to yourself, think to yourself. (long pause) Notice that your attention is not above your ear level but it is more inside rather than outward. (pause) With practice this will help you to focus inward and help you activate your psychic hearing.

Take in three deep breaths. Breathe in through your nose only, and exhale from your mouth. As you are breathing in, visualize a beam of White Light coming down through the top of your head. It can be a bright spot light or a white puffy cloud, however you imagine it.

Let's begin:

Breathe in deeply through your nose and see or feel your magnificent White Light. Exhale through your mouth slowly.

Take another deep breath through your nose and feel the beautiful White Light move down your body. Exhale slowly through your mouth.

Breathe in one more time deeply and hold it, hold it. Exhale quickly through your mouth. You are feeling completely relaxed and rested.

Return to normal breathing and slowly open your eyes. Sit up slowly. Do not talk. Write down everything that you experienced. If you feel dizzy after any meditation or visualization, close your eyes and take another few deep breaths and tell yourself to come straight back into your body.

Write down everything that you experienced during the meditation and visualization.

Meditation Journal

Day _____ **Time** _____

_____

_____

_____

_____

_____

Clairaudience

_____
_____
_____
_____
_____
_____
_____
_____
_____

Exercise 22
Clairaudient

✔❑   You will need blank white paper and a pen or pencil.

✔❑   Go outside, take your pad of paper and pencil. Do not talk. Walk around for about 10 minutes.

✔❑   Pick out separate sounds, such as a single bird, the wind in the trees, water, cars going by, truck sounds, horns beeping, children shouting and playing, or any sounds. Listen intently to each sound.

✔❑   Write down each separate sound that you hear. Try to do this exercise several times a week.

✔❑   Choose a sound, like a robin singing or a baby cooing, to bring forth pleasant happy thoughts and feelings.

✔❑   Choose a sound that reminds you of your childhood and allow yourself to drift back to a happy experience. Write it down in your journal.

Sounds create an atmosphere that we are not consciously aware of. Grating sounds or perhaps large truck sounds could be stimulating sad or angry feelings. We generally walk around oblivious to the sounds that bombard us. They begin to blend together and become just noise. By practicing this simple exercise you will begin to appreciate the beautiful sounds of the Earth as well as the annoying ones. You will also start to recognize the pleasant sounds and pick them out instinctively from the other noise that surrounds us day and night.

Sounds I Heard:

_____
_____
_____
_____

Clairaudience

Exercise 23
Making your own sounds

Being a musical child and later a professional musical comedy and opera singer, I took it for granted that everyone heard the same sounds I did. It became quite apparent that the majority of people do not pay attention to or feel their own inner sounds. Throughout the years, I have found this particular exercise to be extremely beneficial to my students, especially when they realized they could make sounds that they had never felt in their bodies.

My experience of teaching a deaf child to feel sounds made me even more aware of how important it is to hear our own individual voice. You might discover yourself bursting into tears or filled with joy when you begin to release the pent up sounds within your secret world.

✔❑ Find a quiet place, like the beach, your car, or shower. A place that you will feel free to scream if you like.

✔❑ Begin to hum, with your lips tightly closed. Do this for a few minutes. Make the sound mmmmm.........

✔❑ Put your hands on your chest and repeat the mmmmmm sound.

✔❑ Take a deep breath and relax.

✔❑ Now, you are going to sing through your nose with the sounds of nnnnn........like no! Then sing, no, no, no, on one note. Your nose may tickle, this means you are doing it correctly.

✔❑ Make the nnnnnnnn.......no sound again and put your hand on your nose and feel the vibration.

✔❑ These will give you the sensation and vibration of sound throughout your entire body.

✔❑ Then try singing a familiar song, like "Jingle Bells," or one of your favorites. Not only will you feel wonderful after this but you will become more aware of listening and feeling your own individual voice.

Everything has its own voice or sound. It is the way the universe speaks.

Clairaudience

Becoming Your Animal

Exercise 24
Becoming your animal

✔❑ Write down the first animal, mammal, bird, that comes into your mind.

_____

✔❑ Write down the animal, mammal, bird, you would like to be in this life, if you had a choice.

_____

✔❑ Compare the two and see if they are the same?

  ✔❑ Yes ✔❑ No

✔❑ Write a few sentences about that animal, mammal or bird and why you like it so much.

_____
_____
_____
_____
_____
_____
_____
_____
_____

Clairaudience

Write down the sounds it makes.

_____
_____
_____
_____
_____

What color and type of skin does your animal have?

_____
_____
_____
_____
_____
_____

Write down how it travels.

_____
_____
_____
_____
_____
_____
_____

By understanding that animal part of us we will begin to get in touch with our inner nature. That part of us that we deny so much in our everyday living.

✔❑ Cut out a picture of your animal, mammal or bird and put it on your bathroom mirror. Each day this week, I want you to playact or imitate your animal. Walk around like your animal, do the things your animal does. For example: if you are a porpoise, swim in a pool and imitate the sounds and the way the porpoise behaves. If you don't have a pool, try the tub or the floor. Try to respond like your animal.

It will be fun to act out your animal being, for you will soon discover parts of you that you never knew existed.

Clairaudience

✔❏ Write out your experiences as your animal.

1st day: _____
_____
_____
_____

2nd day: _____
_____
_____
_____

3rd day: _____
_____
_____
_____

4th day: _____
_____
_____
_____

5th day: _____
_____
_____
_____

6th day: _____
_____
_____
_____

7th day: _____
_____
_____
_____

Chapter 21

Say Bye-Bye to That Stress

"The mind talks to the body and the body talks back and sometimes it is a fatal conversation."
Russian proverb

Constant stress is bad for you. Health experts now call it the deadliest environmental toxin of this age. Stress is usually misunderstood. It is somehow taken to mean that one is inept at dealing with life or that one is weak and just "doesn't have it!" We also assume it's common to us all rather than subjective to each one alone in our own uniqueness.

Generally we believe that stress is the direct product of those events occurring outside the person rather than within the mental and emotional states of the person and our responses to those events.

Our stress is a response from within to occurrences which seem to threaten our security, stability, status, and even identity. It deals not only with the external events in our lives but also those events within our emotional and mental states and personal reality. It is more likely that we produce a stress response to the events within our minds than to those which simply occur outside us.

We have a tendency to create within our mind ideas and images of what it is we are, the nature of that with which we deal, and even the scripting of events which we "believe" are about to happen next or which "should" or must happen next.

Concentrating on these future activities, and the uncertainty they bring up, creates doubt and fear within the conscious mind. These future activities get "stuck" because the answers lie in the subconscious mind.

Our stress causes the fight-or-flight response, which is the body's physical preparation to cope with what threatens our well-being. Our hormones flood through our systems; our breath becomes quick and shallow; we break out in a sweat; our hearts beat faster. If we have stress in moderation, it can be a lifesaving response that helps us move and think fast. But in excess, we become over-stressed and this can lead to illness.

Stress Triggers

Each person has unique stress triggers: relationships, boredom, memories, physical threats from the environment. Even though stress feels like only an emotion, its lifelong effects are destructive: heart disease, substance abuse, stroke, injury, ulcers, chronic - fatigue syndrome, low back ache, breast pain, depression, and even bad breath. The immune system becomes less effective and many experts suspect stress makes cancer and infectious diseases more likely to take hold. You have to stop this from happening to you. Stress and anxiety are associated with a brain wave production above 21 cycles per second. When our brain activity is greater than 21 cycles per second, the mechanism that

Say Bye-Bye to That Stress

controls the envelope of outer immunity that every normal person has is depleted and the germ virus community that is ever-present is in some manner invited in.

Hospitals and Clinics

Numerous hospitals and clinics across the country are using techniques to combat stress. Tension-both mental and muscular-can complicate the treatment of any disease. Relaxation exercises like imagery, deep breathing, progressive muscle relaxation and meditation help reduce tension and anxiety. A study was done on patients who used the relaxation techniques to de-stress prior to surgery. They discovered that these patients had a speedier recovery and less postoperative pain, reduced their medication, and just felt better all around when compared to a group who did nothing.

Retrain Your Mind

Retraining your mind to think only positive thoughts and images on a moment-to moment basis also helps to reduce the negative physiological effects of the stress response. The basic nature of the mind is to think and imagine constantly. My question to you is, what are the contents of your thoughts? If negative images are always played over and over in your mind, you will suffer the consequences in your body. I see this pattern over and over with my clients.

The fight-or-flight response is solely triggered by your perception, not reality. Suppose you caught sight of a shadow in a corner and thought it was someone hiding, ready to grab you. Your heart will race, your breath will quicken, and you'll break out in a sweat. But if you saw the shadow and realized that it was the tall overstuffed chair, your body would remain calm.

What this means is that if in your daily living you constantly perceive "shadows," your body will respond accordingly, gearing up physically for fight or flight. By using imagery, you can learn to replace negative images with positive ones and give your body a break from all the excess stress.

A good rule to follow though: If an image makes you anxious or apprehensive, don't hesitate to seek out an alternative that eliminates the source of displeasure.

Exercise

Exercise can help interrupt the harmful effects of stress. The muscle action "burns up" the hormones that keyed you up. In other words, when the system has prepared for a fight, exercising gives it what it needs. Exercising also reverses fight-or-flight effects.

Meditation

Meditation is the opposite of exercising and helps you to overcome stress by cutting "the self destructive chatter" between your thought patterns and cellular reaction. Meditation affects a system that works without your conscious control-the autonomic nervous system. One function of the autonomic nervous system is to rev you up for a fight. But realization turns on the opposite function, the one that keeps you on an even keel when there is no threat. Meditation lowers your pulse, blood pressure, breathing rate, and metabolism. Although survival depends on your nervous system being fired up when times are wild, health comes from calmly flowing along the rest of the time. Meditation opens that flow. It's just the relief a tense mind/body requires to live a healthy happy life.

Say Bye-Bye to That Stress

Mental Fine-Tuning

Your body, your mind and your soul all face significant challenge during this growing process. To meet these challenges with focused, positive energy, you need to be mentally fit. If your body is mildly out of condition, you can take steps on your own to regain physical fitness. On the other hand, if your body is in poor physical condition, you should begin by consulting with a physician for guidance about how to improve your physical health without risking greater injury. Similarly, the degree of mental discomfort you may be experiencing determines whether self-help alone can solve your problem or whether you should seek professional guidance.

How's Your Mental State?

Are you really healthy? To determined where you are on a mental fitness continuum, answer the questions in the accompanying chart, Are You Going Sane? If you answer yes to most questions, congratulations; you are among the select group that is considered mentally fit. If your answers are not as positive as you would like, you can take action to build a more comfortable mindset. If you answer no more often than yes, then you may want to find a professional counselor with whom you can talk. Often, just talking about the obstacles in your life will help to resolve them.

Are You Going Sane?

_____Do you have a positive image of yourself and other people? Do you have more happy thoughts than negative ones?

_____Do you wake up each morning feeling good? Are you excited and full of positive anticipation when you think of the day ahead?

_____Do you meet each new task or problem as an opportunity or lesson rather than an obstacle almost impossible to surmount?

_____Do you laugh a lot and maintain your sense of humor even when life gets heavy?

_____Do you rarely feel irritated or express anger toward those around you?

_____Do you take responsibility for who you are and what happens to you rather than placing blame on others or fate?

_____Do you feel grateful for your life circumstances, friends and family, rather than playing the "poor me" role?

_____Are you able to think clearly, and communicate in a clear, open way?

_____Do you have the energy to complete the day? If you miss a night's sleep, can you continue to function?

_____Do you have goals or a vision of the future that you have every intention of achieving?

Say Bye-Bye to That Stress

Stressors and Mental Discomfort

Stress is frequently a catalyst for both minor and major mental discomfort. The more stressors present in your life, the more your mental fitness is affected. To understand the source of emotional or mental distress in your life, take a look at your lifestyle; notice which parts are working poorly and creating stress for you. The following stress factors can impair your mental state.

* **Emotional stress** — an unhappy relationship with a lover or a friend; no close friends, especially one who servers as confidant; poor interactions with family and siblings.

* **Mental stress** — heavy work pressure; not enough time for yourself to be alone and quiet; feeling scattered due to many demands on your time.

* **Social stress** — no close group of friends; pressure from your social group to act in certain ways that
make you uncomfortable; too many social demands and distractions.

* **Environmental stress** — no space of your own, lost of noise and confusion contaminants, such as smoke in the air.

* **Physical stress** — overdoing or under doing physical exercise; allotting exceptional time or energy to sports or other activities.

* **Health stress** — inappropriate types or amounts of alcohol or other drugs; too much caffeine, sugar, junk food, highly processed or fast food; not enough water (six to eight glasses a day); and finally, and very important, lack of a nutritionally well-balanced diet, especially without vitamin or mineral supplements to fill in the nutritional gaps.

On the following page is a list of stress signs.

> **Caution: Some of these symptoms could indicate something other than stress response and you are lovingly encouraged to check your symptoms with the appropriate health-care professional.**

This checklist is very close to a checklist for the disorder of Candida. Stress is a cumulative function as are allergies. Stress can be the result of uncertainties. Change can initiate stress. Reduce the cumulative stress; this will then reduce the resistance to change.

Say Bye-Bye to That Stress

Check those that apply

_____ Overreacting to a small irritation

_____ "Never enough time" syndrome

_____ Wanting to run away

_____ Poor short-term memory

_____ Clenching fist, wringing hands

_____ Frequent sighing or loud exhaling

_____ Skin eruptions, itching or rashes

_____ Cold extremities (feet, hands)

_____ Feeling "about to cry"

_____ Inability to sustain clear thoughts

_____ Running at top speed "on the inside"

_____ Inability to voice emotional complaints

_____ Temporary sexual dysfunction

_____ Weight changes (gain or loss)

_____ Shoulders tense, stiff, sore

_____ Frequent headaches and heartburn

_____ Eyes feel strained, sandy, sore

_____ Difficulty managing feelings or emotions; becoming emotionally numb

_____ Poor coordination; tendency to be accident prone

_____ Sleep problems, feeling tired, fatigue, restless sleep, unusual or disturbing dreams

_____ Inability to recognize stress or to relax: feeling keyed up or weary all the time

_____ Breathlessness, not exhaling, holding one's breath, shallow breathing

_____ Depression, fear, anguish, "I knew it!" or "What's the use!"

_____ Feeling punished, deprived, set aside, rejected, unwanted

_____ Difficulty clearing throat, voice high pitched or often raspy

_____ Feelings of "wanting to hide," "to not be seen," or "having your secret fears or feelings known"

_____ Difficulty in thinking clearly, concentrating or solving problems

_____ Dietary changes, bingeing on junk food or loading up on specific food types

_____ Increasing of use of stimulants such as alcohol, drugs, cigarettes, soda pop

_____ Feelings of alienation: hurt, separation, unworthiness

_____ Small amounts of hair loss, hair tone lacking luster, scalp itch

_____ Blood pressure problems, buzzing in ears, flush head and neck

_____ TOTAL

NOTE: If your total exceeded more than five then we need some serious work.

Say Bye-Bye to That Stress

How to Handle Stress

If you find yourself or a family member or client with these behaviors approach the individual in a non judgmental manner. Describe the behaviors that you are seeing without being accusatory.

**"The person under stress has to recognize that stress is a problem
and figure out what might be causing it"**

* Encourage them to express their feelings of frustration without taking it personally. Become a good listener.

* Help that person to get away from the pressures of home or work for a short time.

* Make sure that they are eating a balanced meal regularly.

* Encourage regular exercise. Deep breathings, visualization or relaxing with music can also do a lot to relieve stress.

* Help them to learn how to prioritize their problems. It helps to focus on those things that they can do something about.

"Provide reassurance that it is OK to let go of things beyond their control."

Visualization - Looking at a Stressful Situation

Let's begin with the Meditation Process in Chapter 4 then continue with the following.

On your blank white movie screen, choose the most stressful situation that you have in your life, remember choose the first situation that comes to you.

Look at this situation and step right in the middle of the stressful problem. (pause) Look around at the others, if others are involved. (pause) Look at what the others are doing and saying to you. (pause)

Observe yourself and how you are experiencing this. Do you like the feeling? Are you feeling trapped, pressured? (pause)

Look at your body. How is it behaving? (Pause) Is your stomach in knots? (pause) Are you ready to scream or cry? (pause)

Now, take three large steps backward stepping away from the stressful situation. Look back at the situation as an observer. (pause)

Choose how you would like this stressful situation resolved. (pause) See yourself talking to the others involved and rectifying the problem. (pause)

Say Bye-Bye to That Stress

Smile, hug, kiss, shake hands, or whatever is appropriate to the others involved. Walk into another room where you feel wonderful, exhilarated, and free from this gnawing stress that has lingered for so long. (pause)

It is time to take in your three deep breaths. Remember breathing in through your nose only, and exhaling from your mouth. As you are breathing in, visualize a beam of White Light coming down through the top of your head. It can be a bright spot light, or a white puffy cloud, however you imagine it.

Let's begin:

Breathe in deeply through your nose and see or feel your magnificent White Light. Exhale through your mouth slowly.

Take another deep breath through your nose and feel the beautiful White Light move down your body. Exhale slowly through your mouth.

Breathe in one more time deeply and hold it, hold it. Exhale quickly through your mouth.

You are feeling completely relaxed and free of pain.

Return to normal breathing and slowly open your eyes. Sit up slowly. Do not talk. Write down everything that you experienced. If you feel dizzy after any meditation or visualization close your eyes and take another few deep breaths and tell yourself to come straight back into your body.

Write down everything that you experienced during the meditation and visualization.

Meditation Journal

Day _____ **Time** _____

_____
_____
_____
_____
_____
_____
_____
_____
_____
_____
_____
_____
_____
_____

Say Bye-Bye to That Stress

STRESS REDUCING SUGGESTIONS

♥ **With Your Body**
- ☆ Exercise regularly.
- ☆ Maintain good posture.
- ☆ Deep breathing, visualization, and meditation.
- ☆ Eat balanced meals regularly.
- ☆ Increase water intake to at least six to eight glasses daily.
- ☆ Get enough sleep and visit your doctor regularly.
- ☆ Reduce sugar, alcohol, caffeine, salt, and nicotine intakes.

♥ **With Your Attitude**
- ☆ Learn to laugh at yourself.
- ☆ Allow yourself to receive hugs daily and give others the same-touching is essential.
- ☆ Learn to express your feelings of frustration.
- ☆ It's OK to let go of things beyond your control.
- ☆ Re-examine that which you hold sacred and true.
- ☆ Realize that the aging process is a part of all of us and we need to learn to accept it joyfully.
- ☆ Be open to advice from others.

♥ **With Your Mind**
- ☆ Prioritize your "to do" list and do the most important ones first.
- ☆ Write your dreams and fantasies in a journal and seek to share them with others, if possible.
- ☆ Focus on those things that you can do something about.
- ☆ Learn to distinguish your own truths from others or outside systems which are influencing you.
- ☆ Live in the present and don't dwell in the past or in the future.
- ☆ Learn to see what is going on around you rather than what you feel, think, or believe is happening.

♥ **With Your Behavior**
- ☆ Get away from the pressures of home or work for a short time-like a mini vacation.
- ☆ Examine whether or not you need a frustrating person in your life.
- ☆ Seek out spiritual connections and commonalties with others.
- ☆ Learn to say "No" to others as well as to your own habits and compulsions.
- ☆ Seek to complete projects or agree not to do them.
- ☆ Learn different skills and talents to help you deal more effectively with changes.
- ☆ Take time daily to stop and reflect on what you are feeling.
- ☆ Unburden yourself of being super-person, super-mom, or super-dad.
- ☆ Learn to listen to what is really being said, not what you expect to be said.
- ☆ Say only what you mean and mean what you say. Also, know that it is OK to not say anything.
- ☆ Forgive and forget grudges, fears, anger, resentments, and jealousies.
- ☆ Understand that your own uniqueness is alright.
- ☆ Learn to mange your money.
- ☆ Meet new people rather than staying with the old safe and familiar friends.

Say Bye-Bye to That Stress

If you are not living your life for you.......then who is? Is it time to make some changes and seek greater quality for you and those with whom you share your life?

Exercise 25
Looking at your perception

One of the things we need to look at is how each of us perceives the world. Each and every one of you perceive things in a unique and wonderful way, influenced highly by your own experiences. What you may see and what your friend, husband, wife, or child may see could be quite different, as is evident when an eyewitness describes what occurred at the scene of a crime or accident. As we grow and change, so do our perceptions of the world.

One of the ways to broaden your perception is to read about or listen to the varied experiences of others, just as we advise in this workbook. By listening to others, you will come to the realization that these experiences are possible.

By expanding your perception of the world, you will begin to increase all of your senses and sharpen your sixth sense allowing you to become more effective in your creative visualizations.

✔❏ Pay attention to what you are aware of and unaware of. What attracts your attention and what do you rarely pay attention to.

✔❏ Do you remember what your wife or husband had on this morning? What did you have for dinner last night?

✔❏ When you find yourself drawn to something, begin to ask why. Is it an opportunity for you or could it be a threat to your job, house, or relationship.

✔❏ It is very important to understand why your mind has learned to focus on whatever it wants you to see.

✔❏ Take a drive, sit and have lunch, go shopping with a friend or loved one.

✔❏ Each make a list below of what you saw on your excursion, describe in detail your surroundings. List sounds, smells, buildings, people, animals, everything you can recall.

Say Bye-Bye to That Stress

My Perceptions

Day _____ **Time** _____

The First Things I Noticed:

_____
_____
_____
_____
_____
_____
_____
_____
_____
_____
_____
_____
_____
_____
_____
_____

Was Anything Missing?

_____
_____
_____
_____
_____
_____
_____
_____
_____
_____

Chapter 22

Predicting Stocks, Newspaper Headlines, Telephone Calls

Exercise 26
Predicting stocks

When you write down your predictions, you probably will not have any emotional feeling about them. But you may begin to experience different sensations, either in your hands or other places in your body. When I am predicting, my hands will begin to tingle just a bit. I first begin to feel anxious and furiously look around for a pad and pencil to write with.

✔❏   Take in your three deep breaths and cover yourself in **White Light**. Bring up your blank white screen, close your eyes to help to cut down all the external distractions or, if it is awkward, keep your eyes open.

✔❏   Don't try to feel, just relax and let the impressions come over to you.

✔❏   Examine a list of stocks on the Stock Exchange listed in your newspaper. Run your fingers over the list and select stocks that might feel right to you. Sometimes your finger will get hot or you might feel a chill up your spine. You will begin to recognize your signals. Keep track of the stock and your scores.

Stock	Today's Date	Today's Price	Price after 1 Week

Predicting

When writing down your predictions, you probably will not have any emotional feelings about them. But you may begin to experience different sensations, either in your hands or other places in your body.

✔❑ Predict the future. Each morning write down what letters the mailman will deliver to you. Sit down, close your eyes, take in your three deep breaths and bring in the *White Light*. Bring up your blank white screen and see who has sent mail to you. Keep records on your score.

Today's Date	Semder	Correct?

Exercise 28
Predicting headlines

✔❑ Close your eyes, take your three deep breaths and bring in the *White Light*. See your blank white screen before reading the morning or evening paper and see if you can tell what the headlines are about. You can even choose a certain section and predict the next days news. Keep score.

Today's Date	Headline	Correct?

141

Predicting

Exercise 29
Predicting phone calls

✔❏   When the phone rings try to see who is calling. Bring up your blank screen, breath in and cover your self with the *White Light* and see if you can get a picture of who is on the line. Keep a record of the accuracy.

✔❏   Do you know when certain people will call you? Is there a particular feeling or flash of a picture, for you? Keep track of these sensations.

Today's Date	Predicted Caller	Correct?

Exercise 30
Sending telepathic message

✔❏   Send a telepathic message to a loved one, such as bring home a carton of milk or butter. Keep a record of the accuracy.

✔❏   In your mind, put up your blank white screen, bring in the *White Light* and see on your screen what ever you want the person to bring home or to the office. Some of us are better senders than receivers.

Date	Requested Item(s)	Receiver	Actual Items

Predicting

> ## Exercise 31
> ## Your predictions

Chose a time where you won't be interrupted. Write down on a piece of paper the number 1. Now write down the very first thing that comes to your mind. Try not to consciously imagine what will happen today. Let go and it will come to you. Write down the thought or just be a word next to the number 1. Don't question what you write! Don't allow your conscious rational mind to get in the way. Do not change it! It is generally the first fleeting thought that is correct. Do at least four or five predictions. Make it a light happy game for yourself. Constantly check what you have written against daily events. Check your dream log and telepathic flashes to see if there is any correlation.

Day _____ **Time** _____

My Predictions

_____

_____

_____

_____

_____

_____

_____

_____

My Predictions

_____

_____

_____

_____

_____

_____

_____

_____

Chapter 23

Reading a Subject

A reading involves just two people; the reader and the subject. You will be using all the techniques that we have learned so far.

Some may only hear the information, others may feel, or know and then there are those who will see what is going on with the subject on their white screen. What ever way it is presented to you it must feel right and comfortable.

Your impressions or images may be subtle at first, but allow the ideas to flow into your awareness. Verbalize your thoughts and pictures to the subject, letting go of whatever thoughts were there previously.

You may see the images like a dream or they may be symbolic. The subject will give you feedback and you will soon discover whether you are doing a literal or symbolic reading. With time and practice the images will become more accurate and your interpretations will flow into your mind and out of your mouth with greater conviction and freedom.

The subject should relax and listen carefully. I suggest recording all readings as the mind gets excited and you have a tendency to forget what was said.

Remember to accept and interpret even the most fleeting or subtle impressions you receive.

Before going on to our exercises in reading a subject, we need to do our Meditation Process.

Visualization - Controlling Pain

Let's begin with the Meditation Process in Chapter 4 then continue with the following.

On your blank, white movie screen, imagine a bright color, the first color that comes to you.

Look at this bright color and visualize it as a sphere of bright light about six inches in diameter.

See it growing bigger and bigger, until it completely fills your screen. Keep looking at your screen and this beautiful vibrant color. (pause) Now picture the color shrinking, growing smaller and smaller, until it is back to the original size. It is still growing smaller and smaller, until it's only an inch or so in diameter, still shrinking, and finally disappearing completely.

Take in a deep breath through your nose and exhale through your mouth.

Look at your blank white movie screen in front of your closed eyes and this time I want you to imagine that the bright color you saw before is now your pain.

Reading a Subject

See your pain growing bigger and bigger, until it completely fills your screen. Keep looking at your screen and your pain. (pause)

Now picture your pain shrinking, growing smaller and smaller, until it's only an inch or so in diameter, still shrinking, and finally disappearing completely.

*I want you to take in three deep breaths. Breathe in through your nose only, and exhale from your mouth. As you are breathing in, visualize a beam of **White Light** coming down through the top of your head. It can be a bright spot light or a white puffy cloud, however you imagine it.*

Let's begin:

*Breathe in deeply through your nose and see or feel your magnificent **White Light**. Exhale through your mouth slowly.*

*Take another deep breath through your nose and feel the beautiful **White Light** move down your body. Exhale slowly through your mouth.*

Breathe in one more time deeply and hold it, hold it. Exhale quickly through your mouth.

You are feeling completely relaxed and free of pain.

Return to normal breathing and slowly open your eyes. Sit up slowly. Do not talk. Write down everything that you experienced. If you feel dizzy after any meditation or visualization, close your eyes and take another few deep breaths and tell yourself to come straight back into your body.

Write down everything that you experienced during the meditation and visualization.

Meditation Journal

Day _____ **Time** _____

_____
_____
_____
_____
_____
_____
_____
_____
_____
_____
_____
_____
_____

Reading a Subject

Exercise 31
Reading people, places & situations

**After a great deal of practice you will be able to turn on
the *White Light* like a light switch and be ready to read someone.**

Suppose you are in a new job and are asked to come into the bosses office. You are scared, unsure, and feel alone in this new space. Once inside the room you can practice this exercise. Or you could be buying a new house and want to know for sure whether or not this is the right house for you and your family.

This same process can be used for meeting someone new. I generally do this when I meet someone and shake hands with them. I continue to feel their energy as they are talking (don't confuse this with reading what is going on with the person) as to whether or not I want to continue the conversation or strike up a relationship with that person.

Remember, don't be too obvious about your actions, the person may notice something and this will make them feel uncomfortable. And above all, always remember it is necessary to have permission to read someone else's inner thoughts, desires, etc. Don't blurt out, "Gosh, it feels like you are really angry at your wife or husband," or what ever the case may be. People will get very upset with you and back away. We are merely observing an overall sensation to help ourselves decide if this is the situation we want to be in.

You can practice this at home, at work, or in a social function. After a while you will be able to sense how a co-worker is feeling or when to approach your boss about a situation.

✔❑ Take a deep breath and bring in the White Light. You can close your eyes, which helps to cut down all the external distractions or, if it is awkward, keep your eyes open.

✔❑ Don't try to feel, just relax and let the impressions come to you.

Exercise 31
Reading a person

✔❑ **Reader** Have the **subject** sit across from you. Sit either on the floor, making sure to keep your back straight or sit in a comfortable chair again keeping your back straight.

✔❑ Make sure both of your feet are on the floor. Have a pad and pencil on your lap or on a table next to you.

✔❑ Always try to record your readings. You and your subject will get excited and forget what you said, or they could misinterpret what you had explained. The tape will keep everything straight.

✔❑ Put the date and name of your **subject** first on the tape sand then say, "This reading is by........."

Reading a Subject

✔❑ **Reader** Take in your three deep breaths, with your hands open and facing upward on your lap. Remember to flood yourself with the *White Light* and then bring up your blank white screen.

✔❑ Put the paper and pencil in your lap. Write their first name only, in the upper right-hand corner of the pad. Draw pictures if you can't explain it in words.

I have found my yellow 8 1/2 by 11 pad and pencil to be an absolute necessity when doing my readings. Even when I do my radio shows, I write down the person's first name and sometimes will doodle with lines or a picture of some kind while doing my mini-readings on the air. It really helps. My sense is that the lead in the pencil acts as a conduit in helping to tap into the energy of the person you are reading. A picture is worth a thousand words and I have been able to draw what I was seeing and have the client say, "Yes, that's exactly how it is or how it looks."

Our names are very important as well, they were given to us at birth and they hold a certain vibration which we can use as a tool when reading someone. I have had several funny stories on the air when the caller did not give me his or her real name. I will hesitate and ask in a very polite way, "Excuse me, but is this name your Christian name, the name on your birth certificate?" There is always a dead silence and then the voice on the other end says, "Annette, you are incredible. No, that is not my real name." A correct name is given by the caller and I go on from there.

✔❑ **Reader** Allow any thoughts, feelings, pictures, smells, or tastes to come forward. Let the thoughts and pictures come to you. Begin to talk and tell what you are experiencing.

✔❑ **Subject** Give the reader feedback from the beginning and as the reading moves along. It is most important to acknowledge the reader, so he or she feels comfortable they are truly seeing or feeling something about the subject.

✔❑ If the **reader** is having trouble experiencing anything, **subject** ask questions about certain areas of your life, such as, "How do you see my career going? Should I change jobs? Should I move? How is my relationship with my husband, wife or ....? I always ask my clients at the beginning of the reading, "What area of your life do you want me to look at?" Then I list them on the right hand side of my yellow pad. You can do the same if you find it easier this way.

✔❑ **Only do this exercise for 15 minutes or shorter** if the reader appears to be frustrated, tired, or anxious.

✔❑ **Reader** Close your hands making a fist. Take in two deep breaths and cover yourself with the beautiful *White Light*... On the third breath exhale quickly and open your hands. Open your eyes and relax.

✔❑ **Subject** Give the reader instant feedback. Remember the reader may have been seeing things in a symbolic way, so it is most important to talk about what he or she saw, felt, or thought was the situation.

We learn through feedback, which I feel is one of the most important aspects of becoming a good psychic reader. Remember practice makes perfect!

Reading a Subject

Reading

Day _____ **Time** _____

Name of subject:

_____
_____
_____
_____
_____
_____
_____
_____
_____
_____
_____
_____
_____
_____
_____
_____
_____
_____
_____
_____
_____
_____
_____
_____
_____
_____
_____
_____
_____
_____

Reading a Subject

Feedback

Day _____ **Time** _____

Name of subject:

_____
_____
_____
_____
_____
_____
_____
_____
_____
_____
_____
_____
_____
_____
_____
_____
_____
_____
_____
_____
_____
_____
_____
_____
_____
_____
_____
_____
_____
_____
_____
_____

Congratulations
You made it to graduation day.

Now that you have successfully completed this *"Discovering Your Psychic World"* workbook you will find that the skills you have learned will become invaluable. You will sense things that you never sensed before. You will begin to recognize the hidden elements behind the spoken words. You will know things about others that will guide you in your decision making. Dreams will be more meaningful and understood.

There is no limit to how far you can go in your exploration of your sixth sense or psychic ability. The only limitations will be the ones you set up in your life. Believe in yourself, act and think positively, and your self confidence will grow beyond your imagination. Yet always be patient, kind, and above all listen to others.

We have assisted in teaching you courage and how to act on your own intuitive convictions. Now it is up to you. The more you search, the more you will find.

May the White Light Be with You

Appendix A

Notes on Professional Ethics

1. Obtain a business license at the City Hall of your town. I have found the city fathers prefer to have a name like mine: Institute of Intuitive Research.

2. Federal & State Id no. for payroll taxes.

3. Insurance, (compensation, professional therapist insurance).

4. Profession should be confined to working hours or evenings during the regular work week. If you do not follow this procedure you will find yourself getting very tired and resentful of people taking up your weekend time.

5. Do not offer your services if they are not desired or wanted.

6. Never, but never go up to someone and tell them about themselves, whether it is good news or bad. This puts people off and makes them feel as if they have no secrets. You must only do the readings when asked.

7. When friends and acquaintances call for a <u>free reading</u>, they should be informed of your office hours if they wish to book an appointment. Throughout my many years of practice, I have found that if I give a free reading the person does not listen and take it in wholeheartedly. They will have a tendency to brush it off. I have always contended, even if you have no money, an exchange is better.

8. Don't be taken or led into or chided by news media or anyone else by absurd questions or games. State firmly, but lovingly that you take your profession seriously and do not consider it a game.

9. Dealing with the "How accurate are you?" statement is a difficult one and should be handled with poise and care......not anger! Give them an example but don't be arrogant or defensive in your statement.

10. Do not sell or submit your mailing list to anyone!!!!!!!! Many people do not wish others to know they went to see a psychic. I have a release form that all my clients sign and on the bottom I ask them if they would like to be on my mailing list. I also have a form that explains what I do, this saves time when we start the reading.

11. Your attitude should always be positive and loving. Remember you are only suggesting what they might do for themselves. It is up to the client to take it from there.

12. Always use the *White Light* and clear yourself after each reading. You do not want to hold onto any of your clients garbage. There is no need for you to remember their problems and try to solve them with your rational mind. Once you have done the reading it is over! Let go of the information!

13. Have a space where you do your readings, such as an office or special place in your home. Do not sit behind a desk, client will feel isolated from you. Sit across from them. Decorate your space with nice artifacts and soft colors. Do not burn incense or have heavy smells around. This is offensive to people and many are allergic to these type of odors.

14. And last of all, **It is not what you say, but how you say it**, that counts!

Glossary

ACUPUNCTURE: An ancient Chinese system of medicine that used needles inserted in the body at prescribed sites to stimulate the flow of chi (life energy) and thereby allegedly restore balance to the energy system that is thought to determine health. Modern variants of the original system use sound, lasers, chemicals, and massage on the acupuncture points.

AGENT: In telepathy tests, the sender, or person whose mental states are to be apprehended by the percipient or receiver. In GESP tests, the person who looks at the target object. In spontaneous cases of ESP phenomena, the person who apparently initiates telepathic communication. In RSPK, the apparent initiator or focal point for poltergeist occurrences.

ALTERED STATE OF CONSCIOUSNESS (ASC): A pattern of awareness that is qualitatively different in overall mental functioning from one's ordinary waking pattern.

ANPSI: PSI in animals.

APPARITION: A visual paranormal appearance, generally spontaneous, that suggests the real presence of someone distant or dead.

APPORT: An object that purportedly appears in a closed area, indicating the apparent penetration of matter by matter, that is, de-materialization of an object that passes through obstacles, such as walls, and then re-materializes.

ASC: See Altered State of Consciousness.

ASTRAL BODY: A hypothetical replica, or "double," of the individual's physical body that is exact but nonphysical. It is said to be the vehicle which leaves the physical body in OOBE.

ASTRAL PROJECT 10: See out-of-body experiences.

AURA: An envelope or field of colored energy or radiation (is said by sensitives to surround the human body with the color or colors indicative of different aspects of the person's physical, psychological, and spiritual condition.) Some traditions hold that there is more than one aura within the total envelope, each having distinctive properties.

AUTOMATIC WRITING: Writing done as a motor automatism in a dissociated state, that is, not under conscious control of the writer.

AUTOMATISM: Any sensory or motor activity carried out by a person in a dissociated state or without conscious muscular effort or mental direction.

BASIC TECHNIQUE (BT): The clairvoyance-testing technique in which each card is laid aside by the experimenter as it is called by the subject. At the end of the run, the checkup is made.

BILOCATION: The apparent simultaneous presence of a person in two different locations by paranormal means-generally thought to involve an astral double.

BIOCOMMUNICATIONS: A Russian term for telepathy.

BIOENERGETICS: A Russian term for psychokinesis.

BIOFEEDBACK: An instrumental technique for self-monitoring of normally unconscious, involuntary body processes such as brain waves, heartbeat rate, and muscle tension that can result in a degree of conscious, voluntary control of the process.

BIOINFORMATION: A Russian term for extrasensory perception.

Glossary

BIOLOCATION: A Russian term for clairvoyance.

BIOPLASMA: A hypothetical form of energy purportedly associated with living organisms, demonstrated by some Soviet researchers through Kirlian photography and termed by them "a fourth state of matter."

BT: See Basic Technique.

CALL: The specific guess made by the subject in trying to identify a target in an ESP test.

CHANCE: The complex of undefined factors irrelevant to and uncorrelated with the purpose at hand.

CHANCE EXPECTATION (MEAN CHANCE EXPECTATION): In testing for psychic phenomena, the most likely score if no information transfer is involved.

CLAIRAUDIENCE: Extrasensory data perceived as sound.

CLAIRSENTIENCE: An archaic term meaning extra sensory awareness in a general sense as distinguished from the visual mode clairvoyance), auditory mode (clairaudience), and other sensory modes.

CLAIRVOYANCE: ESP of physical objects or events as distinguished from telepathy, which involves ESP of thoughts.

COMMUNICATOR: An ostensible discarnate personality said to communicate with the living, usually through a medium or sensitive.

CONTROL: In trance mediumship, the ostensible discarnate personality of intelligence that habitually messages or originates communications through a medium to a sitter. Some researchers interpret this as a dissociation effect- that is, a secondary, repressed personality of the sensitive.

CONSCIOUSNESS: (1) A state of waking awareness. (2) The fundamental dimension or stratum of existence, through which all mental and physical activity (thoughts, feelings, sensations, dreams, volition, and behavior) is accomplished.

Hence, consciousness is more than self-awareness. So-called unconscious activities also are dependent upon some degree of consciousness.

COSMIC CONSCIOUSNESS: Purportedly the highest state of consciousness known to humans. An awareness of the design and meaning of the universe and life is said to be obtained, along with a feeling of ecstasy, moral and intellectual illumination, and other characteristics generally exemplified by saints and enlightened spiritual teachers.

CRITICAL RATIO (CR): A statistical test used in limited choice tests to determine whether the observed deviation is significantly greater than the expected random fluctuation about the average. The CR is obtained by dividing the observed deviation by the standard deviation. (The probability of a given CR may be obtained by consulting tables of the probability integral.)

CROSS CORRESPONDENCE: A highly complex series of communications through two or more mediums unknown to each other that provides an understandable message only when the separate fragments are put together.

DEATHBED EXPERIENCE: An unusual state of exaltation or altered perception in a dying person, sometimes with apparent awareness of the presence of deceased loved ones.

Glossary

DEJA VU: French for "already seen," The experience in which a new event feels as if it has been experienced before.

DE-MATERIALIZATION: The purported paranormal disappearance, usually quite rapid, of an object.

DEVIATION: In quantitative testing, the amount an observed number of hits or an average score varies (either above or below) from mean chance expectation.

DIRECT VOICE: A phenomenon of mediumship in which an isolated voice without visible source is purportedly heard.

DISCARNATE: Disembodied. Used in mediumistic communications to refer to a soul, intelligence, or personality of a deceased person. In a more general sense it includes the concepts of elementals, nature spirits, and deities.

DISPLACEMENT: ESP responses to targets other than those for which the calls were intended. Displacement may be either forward or backward. Displacement to the targets one, two, three, etc., places after the intended target are designated as (+1), (+2), (+3), etc. Displacement to the targets one, two, three, etc., places before the intended target are designated (-1), (-2), (-3), etc.

DISSOCIATION: A splitting of the mind so that one or more parts behave independently of the other, each functioning as a separate unit.

DOUBLE: The purported astral or etheric counterpart of the physical body said to temporarily move about in space and appear in various degrees of density to others.

DOWSING: A form of clairvoyance in which underground water, minerals, or hidden objects are located apparently by means of a divining (dowsing) rod, pendulum, or other instrument.

DOWN THROUGH (DT): The clairvoyance technique in which the cards are called down through the pack before any are removed or checked.

ECTOPLASM: A semi-physical substance alleged to issue from the body of a physical medium and out of which materialization's are sometimes formed.

ESP: See Extrasensory Perception.

ESP CARDS (ZENER CARDS): Cards that bear one of these symbols: star, circle, square, cross, and waves (three parallel wavy lines). A standard pack has 25 cards, five of each symbol.

EXTRASENSORY PERCEPTION (ESP): The experience of, or response to, an external event, object, state, or influence without contact through the known senses. ESP is sometimes unconscious, that is, it occurs without awareness of it by the person or people involved, as in psi-mediated instrumental responses (PMIR).

FC: See Field Consciousness.

FIELD CONSCIOUSNESS (FC): An ASC in which an individual seems to experience an enlargement of the ordinary boundaries of self, so that part or all of the individual's environment becomes merged with his awareness of self.

GENERAL EXTRASENSORY PERCEPTION (GESP): ESP that could be either telepathy or clairvoyance, or both.

GHOST: The popular term for an apparition of a deceased person.

Glossary

GUIDE: A benevolent, protective super-mundane influence alleged to continually watch over a person.

HALLUCINATION: A visual or auditory experience similar to sense perception but without sensory stimulation. It is termed vertical when it corresponds to a real event taking place outside the range of sensory awareness.

HAUNTING: Paranormal phenomena associated with a certain location, especially a building. The phenomena are usually attributed to the activity of discarnate spirits.

HIGH-VOLTAGE PHOTOGRAPHY: Photography that characteristically uses a pulsed high-frequency electrical field and two electrodes, between which are placed the object to be photographed and an unexposed film plate. No optics are involved. It is also possible to gain this effect with direct current (DC) and/or low-frequency pulses. If a transparent electrode is used, the film may be placed outside.

HIT: A correct response in a test for some aspect of PSI.

HYPERESTHESIA: Usually sensitivity of the skin or a particular sense.

ILLUSION: An erroneous interpretation of sensory data obtained normally.

INTUITION: The ability of knowing, or the knowledge obtained, without conscious recourse to inference or reasoning.

KIRLIAN PHOTOGRAPHY: A type of high-voltage photography.

KUNDALINI: According to yogic philosophy, a nonphysical energy in the human body, derived from prana, which is capable of activating psychic centers called chakras. Its activation in individuals through practice of various spiritual disciplines is said to result in enlightenment, genius, creativity, and psychic powers. Thought by some modern investigators, such as Gopi Krishna, to be the psycho physiological mechanism by which the human race evolves towards higher consciousness.

LEVITATION: The purported raising of objects or bodies in the air by no apparent physical means.

MATERIALIZATION: A purported paranormal event in which some forms or objects become suddenly visible in solid form. Some physical mediums claim to use ectoplasm for materialization's. Other types of psychics are said to materialize known physical objects such as coins or buttons that are indistinguishable from the genuine articles.

MEAN CHANCE EXPECTATION: See Chance Expectation.

MEDIUM: A sensitive who apparently perceives and communicates with discarnates, or who acts as a channel for discarnates to communicate through direct voice. A mental medium receives messages from the deceased and transmits them to the living. A physical medium can, in addition, produce physical effects such as levitation and materialization.

MISS: An erroneous response in a test for some aspect of PSI.

MYSTICISM: The doctrine or belief that direct knowledge of God or ultimate reality is attainable through intuition or insight and in a way differing from ordinary sense perception or the use of logical reasoning.

NEURAL: The adjectival form of neuron.

NEURON: The fundamental functional unit of the nervous system.

Glossary

NOETICS: The general study of consciousness; from the Greek root nous, "mind."

OBJECT READING: See Psychometry.

OMEGA: The symbol for consciousness and noetics.

PARAPHYSICS: The study of the physics of paranormal processes, that is, phenomena that resemble physical phenomena but are without recognizable physical cause.

PARANORMAL: As related to psychic research, faculties and phenomena that are beyond "normality" in terms of cause and effect as currently understood.

PARAPSYCHOLOGY: The branch of science that deals with ESP and PK, that is, behavioral or personal exchanges with the environment that are extra-sensorimotor (not dependent on the senses and muscles).

PERCIPIENT: A subject in an ESP test or a person who has a spontaneous ESP experience.

PHANTASM OF THE DEAD: An apparition or appearance suggesting the presence of a person or animal no longer living.

PHANTASM OF THE LIVING: An apparition or appearance suggesting the presence of a living person or animal that is not there.

PK: See Psychokinesis.

PLACEMENT TEST: A technique for testing PK in which the subject tries to influence falling objects to land in a designated area of the surface on which they are thrown.

PMIR: See Psi-Mediated Instrumental Response.

POLTERGEIST: German for "noisy spirit." Various paranormal manifestations involving the unexplained movement or breakage of objects. Poltergeist activity differs from a haunting in that it often seems to center around the presence of an adolescent. Now generally termed recurrent spontaneous psychokinesis (RSPK).

POSSESSION: A state in which a person seems to be under the control in mind and body of another personality, generally thought to be a discarnate (and sometimes non-human) spirit.

PRANA: A form of energy postulated in ancient Hindu texts as the basic life force. Prana is thought to exist outside the types of energy (electricity, magnetism, gravity, and the nuclear forces) known to Western science. It conceptually resembles the odic force (Reichenbach), orgone (Reich), chi (acupuncture theory),and bioplasma.

PRIMARY PERCEPTION: A hypothetical sensory system or perception capability allegedly existing in cell life that allows plants and animals low in the evolutionary scale to monitor their environment and communicate with other organisms, including humans.

PROBABILITY: A mathematical statement of the likelihood of occurrence of a particular event, normally expressed as a decimal fraction. In parapsychology literature, probability (P) is a mathematical estimate of the a priori likelihood that chance alone could produce a particular result, while probability (p) the statistically analyzed result of a particular test.

PSI: A term to designate collectively paranormal events and/or faculties, including ESP, PK, and survival phenomena.

Glossary

PSI FIELD: The region in space in which PSI are detectable.

PSI-MEDIATED INSTRUMENTAL RESPONSE (PMIR): The production by the organism of one or more responses that are instrumental in serving the needs of the organism, when these responses are made possible by PSI factors (ESP and/or PK). This can occur without the conscious intention or awareness of the organism.

PSI-MISSING: Use of PSI ability, so that the subject avoids the target he is trying to hit more often than would be expected if only chance were operating.

PSYCHE: The Greek word for soul. In current English usage it can mean soul or mind.

PSYCHIC: (1) A synonym for sensitive. (2) Describing paranormal events and abilities that cannot be explained in terms of established physical principles.

PSYCHIC PHOTOGRAPHY: See thoughtography.

PSYCHIC RESEARCH: A traditional term for the branch of science that studies PSI in the laboratory and in the field.

PSYCHIC SURGERY: A form of healing in which portions of diseased tissues are allegedly removed without the use of instruments.

PSYCHOENERGETICS: A Russian term for parapsychology.

PSYCHOPHYSIOLOGY: The study of mental events as they relate to physiological changes in the body. Often called physiological psychology.

PSYCHO SPHERE: In the philosophy of cosmic humanism, the hyper dimensional field of consciousness whereby the individual reaches up to the Cosmic Imagination (God) and the universal spirit reaches down to man in synchronicity or resonance.

PSYCHOTRONICS: The Czechoslovakian term for parapsychology.

RADIESTHESIA: (1) Sensitivity to radiation's throughout the spectrum of radiation's from any source, living or inert. (2) A synonym for dowsing.

RAPID EYE MOVEMENT (REM): Eye movement by a sleeping person that indicates he is dreaming.

RECURRENT SPONTANEOUS PSYCHOKINETIC PHENOMENA (RSPK): The modern term for poltergeist.

REINCARNATION: A theory of survival in which some aspect of a deceased person is reborn in another human body. Reincarnation is often confused with the transmigration of souls, which allows for rebirth of a human soul in the body of an animal.

REM: See Rapid Eye Movement.

RSPK: See Recurrent spontaneous Psychokinetic Phenomena.

RUN: A group of trials, usually the successive calling of a deck of 25 ESP cards or symbols. In PK tests, a run consists of 24 throws, regardless of the number of dice thrown at the same time.

Glossary

SCORE: The number of hits made in any given unit of trials, usually a run. Total score is the pooled score of all runs. Average score is the total score divided by the number of runs.

SEANCE (SITTING): A meeting of one or more persons with a medium, usually with the object of receiving communications from discarnates through the medium.

SIDDHI: Sanskrit term for psychic power. In yogic philosophy, siddhis may awaken in the course of one's spiritual development but should be ignored because they are a hindrance to attaining enlightenment.

SIGNIFICANCE: A numerical result is significant when it equals or surpasses some criterion of degree or chance improbability. The criterion commonly used in psychic research and parapsychology today is a probability value of 0.05, or odds of 20:1 against chance, or a deviation in either direction such that the CR is 2.33 or greater.

SITTER: A person who consults or sits with a medium or sensitive.

SITTING: See Seance

SPIRIT COMMUNICATION: A communication, usually obtained through a medium or automatic writing, purporting to come from a deceased personality.

SPIRITUALISM: A religious movement with doctrines and practices based on the belief that survival of death is a reality and that communication between the living and the deceased occurs, usually via mediumship.

SUBJECT: The person who is tested in an experiment.

SUBLIMINAL PERCEPTION: Non conscious response to stimuli that are below the threshold of normal awareness.

SURVIVAL: The concept of continued conscious existence for some time after death. Immortality (eternal existence) is neither implied nor ruled out.

SYNCHRONICITY: A term coined by C. G. Jung for meaningful coincidences as a causal connecting principle that could account for some psi.

TARGET: In ESP tests, the objective or mental events to which the subject is attempting to respond. In PK tests, the objective process or object that the subject tries to influence (such as the face or location of a die). A target card is the card that the percipient is attempting to identify or otherwise indicate a knowledge of. A target face is the face of the falling die that the subject tries to make turn up by PK. A target pack is a pack of cards whose order the subject is attempting to identify.

TC: See Transpersonal Consciousness.

TELEPORTATION: A form of psychokinesis similar to telekinesis but generally used to designate the movement of objects (apports) through other physical objects or over great distances.

THETA: (1) The term that collectively designates survival phenomena, from the Greek word thanatos, "death." (2) A type of brain wave.

THOUGHT FORMS: The purported creation of physical forms by mentally projecting an image that materializes in the visible world.

Glossary

THOUGHTOGRAPHY: The paranormal ability to produce images on photographic film.

TOBISCOPE: A portable device for detecting acupuncture points through measuring skin resistance.

TRANCE: An ASC, induced or spontaneous, that gives access to many ordinarily inhibited capacities of the mind-body system. These include imageries, accelerated mental processes, creative automatism, enhanced concentrations and perception, and other important phenomena. There are a variety of trance states, not just a single state.

TRANSPERSONAL CONSCIOUSNESS (TC): Consciousness that extends or goes beyond the personal or individual.

TRANSPERSONAL PSYCHOLOGY: A new major psychological approach to the study of the person that emphasizes humanity's ultimate development or transcendent potential as individuals and a species. Sometimes referred to as the "fourth force" in psychology (the others being psychoanalysis, behaviorism, and humanistic psychology).

TRAVELING CLAIRVOYANCE: An older term used to describe hypnotized subjects' clairvoyance of distant scenes.

TRIAL: In ESP tests, a single attempt to identify a target object. In PK tests, a single unit of effect to be measured in the evaluation of results.

VERIDICAL HALLUCINATION: A hallucination corresponding with some degree of accuracy to an external object, person, place, or event.

ZENNER CARDS: See ESP cards.

Peaceful White Light

3 Audio Cassettes - 6 Guided Meditations
featuring
Annette Martin & the Music of Steven Halpern

"Annette Martin is an acclaimed radio/TV psychic who has been teaching intuitive development for more than 18 years. Her new three audio tape set, Peaceful White Light, features six guided meditations that will guide you through a powerful process in learning how to calm your mind and body. Featuring the beautiful music of Radiance, Crystal Suite and Spectrum Suite by Steven Halpern, this dynamic audio set includes specific exercises and visualization techniques that will help you gain confidence, clarity, solve problems, relieve stress and achieve your most important goals. These superb tapes are a must for those desiring to change their lives! "

Leading Edge Review - Spring '94

MEDITATIONS
- White Light Bubble **(Chapter 4)**
- Inner Guide **(Chapter 9)**
- Reminiscing **(Chapter 13)**
- Magical Garden **(Chapter 6)**
- Loved One **(Chapter 11)**
- Ocean Waves

What Users are Saying.......

"I believe that relaxation and visual imagery are important tools for healing. Annette Martin's Peaceful White Light tape series can be useful at facilitating this for your essential healing process."
Elson M. Haas, MD, Director of Preventive Medical Center of Marin, Inc. author of Staying Healthy with Nutrition

"The effect was wonderful. I have included Peaceful White Light on my packing list so I never am on a flight without it." Lisa Contini, seminar leader

"Hollywood motion picture production and marketing is a stressful business. Annette's tapes prepare me for a challenging day at work. I'm able to relax, center myself and go about creating miracles. It's a powerful experience. "
Cirina Catania, Hollywood Publicist and Marketing Executive

"Since using your meditation tapes I have been able to experience a relaxation level and calmness like never before. A certain sense of "knowing" and "understanding" regarding my patients and life-in-general has increased along with a strong feeling of security." Dr. Charles Decker, Chiropractor

"Annette, your tapes make me feel so good and I am not afraid of the dark anymore." Katlin, four year old

"My mother bought your tapes to help me relax and even my school work has improved." Jake, eleven year old

"I can't sleep without listening to your beautiful Peaceful White Light tapes." Jessie, seven year old

Other Products

Annie Sunshine & the White Owl of the Cedars

Children's Audio Story

"This new Annette Martin audio tape will charm children and the child in you. In order to save the feather clan tribe, Chief Goodmorning must follow the white owl of the cedars to the Sacred Mountain to find an annie and strings of sunshine. There, amid a pile of leaves, he finds a strange baby with blond hair and white skin. The chief names her Annie Sunshine and returns to the camp where Old Crocus Foot attempts to drown Annie Sunshine in the river. Children will learn to trust their feelings and dreams by listening to Annie Sunshine and the White Owl of the Cedars time and again!"

Leading Edge Review - Summer '94

"Annette Martin writes remarkable fairy tales that captivate the hearts of her readers. Annette's voice is magical and her stories bring the myth and wonder of spiritual awareness to engaging fairy tale experiences young reader relate to."

Jerry Gay, Pulitzer Prize Winning Journalist

"A delightful, captivating, beautifully illustrated story. Annette's voice is mesmerizing as she weaves her fairy tale within your consciousness. This would be most appealing to 3rd - 8th grade students. It has the ingredients to spark meaningful discussion between teacher and class regarding prejudices, right vs wrong, perseverance, and belief in self and others."

La Moyne Troedson, Assistant School Superintendent

Side A - The Story
Entertaining and educational.

Side B - Sleepy Time Adventure
Sleepy time adventure to relax and prepare your child for sleep.

Music by the Native American group Red Thunder from their "Red Thunder" CD and international pianist and composer Robert Van Horne in his "China Love" CD

Order Form

Send request to:

Artistic Visions, Inc.
2075 Winchester Blvd. Suite 107
Campbell, CA 95008 - 3432

I would like to order:

	Qty	Price	Total
Peaceful White Light Audio Tapes	_____	$24.95	_____
Discovering Your Psychic World Workbook	_____	$19.95	_____
Annie Sunshine & the White Owl of the Cedars & Sleepy time Adventure Audio Tape	_____	$9.95	_____
Annie Sunshine Story, Color & Activity Book	_____	$2.75	_____
Shipping & Handling ($3.00 for each item)	_____	$3.00	_____
	Total Order		_____
	Sales Tax (California residents add 8.25%)		_____
	Total Amount Due		_____

❑ **Enclosed is my check or money order made out to: Artistic Visions, Inc.**

❑ **Charge my credit card as checked:** ❑ **Visa**   ❑ **Master Card**

Card Number _____ **Expires** _____

Name on Card _____

Signature _____

Send to: (please print clearly)

Name _____

Address _____

City, State, ZIP _____